Everyday

FAMILY MEAL

MAKEOVERS

PUBLISHED IN 2018 BY BAUER MEDIA BOOKS, AUSTRALIA.

BAUER MEDIA BOOKS IS A DIVISION OF BAUER MEDIA PTY LTD.

Bauer Media Books

PUBLISHER
JO RUNCIMAN

EDITORIAL & FOOD DIRECTOR
SOPHIA YOUNG

DIRECTOR OF SALES, MARKETING & RIGHTS
BRIAN CEARNES

EDITORIAL DIRECTOR-AT-LARGE
PAMELA CLARK

CREATIVE DIRECTOR
HANNAH BLACKMORE

MANAGING EDITOR
STEPHANIE KISTNER

SENIOR DESIGNER
JEANNEL CUNANAN

FOOD EDITOR
KATHLEEN DAVIS

JUNIOR EDITOR
AMANDA LEES

OPERATIONS MANAGER
DAVID SCOTTO

PHOTOGRAPHER
BENITO MARTIN

STYLIST
KATE BROWN

PHOTOCHEFS
CARLY SOPHIA TAYLOR, ELIZABETH FIDUCIA

PRINTED IN CHINA
BY LEO PAPER PRODUCTS LTD

A CATALOGUE RECORD FOR THIS
BOOK IS AVAILABLE FROM THE
NATIONAL LIBRARY OF AUSTRALIA.
ISBN: 978-1-74245-987-5

© BAUER MEDIA PTY LIMITED 2018
ABN 18 053 273 546

PUBLISHED BY BAUER MEDIA BOOKS,
A DIVISION OF BAUER MEDIA PTY LTD,
54 PARK ST, SYDNEY; GPO BOX 4088,
SYDNEY, NSW 2001, AUSTRALIA
PH +61 2 9282 8618; FAX +61 2 9126 3702
WWW.AWWCOOKBOOKS.COM.AU

ORDER BOOKS
PHONE 136 116 (WITHIN AUSTRALIA)

OR ORDER ONLINE AT
WWW.AWWCOOKBOOKS.COM.AU

SEND RECIPE ENQUIRIES TO
RECIPEENQUIRIES@BAUER-MEDIA.COM.AU

THE AUSTRALIAN
Women's Weekly

Everyday
FAMILY MEAL

MAKEOVERS

TRIPLE TESTED
THE AUSTRALIAN WOMEN'S WEEKLY
TEST KITCHEN

Contents

PASTA NIGHTS 06

STIR-FRIES 44

SUPER SALADS 82

BEST BAKES 124

MODERN ROASTS 160

DINNER IN A DISH 194

GLOSSARY 232

CONVERSION CHART 237

INDEX 238

MACARONI FARFALLE

RAVIOLI LASAGNE

PENNE

RIGATONI

FETTUCCINE

CANNELLONI

SPAGHETTI

ORZO LINGUINE

ORECCHIETTE

GNOCCHI

FUSILLI

PASTA NIGHTS

SPAGHETTI LENTIL 'BOLOGNESE'

PREP + COOK TIME 30 MINUTES **SERVES** 4

- **2 tablespoons olive oil**
- **1 large onion (200g), chopped finely**
- **2 cloves garlic, crushed**
- **2 tablespoons coarsely chopped fresh basil**
- **1 teaspoon dried oregano leaves**
- **400g (12½oz) canned diced tomatoes**
- **400g (12½oz) canned tomato puree**
- **400g (12½oz) canned brown lentils, drained, rinsed**
- **400g (12½oz) spaghetti**
- **⅓ cup (25g) finely grated pecorino cheese**
- **2 tablespoons small basil leaves, extra**

1 Heat oil in a large deep frying pan over medium heat; cook onion, stirring, for 5 minutes or until golden. Stir in garlic, herbs, diced tomatoes and puree; cook for 5 minutes. Add lentils, then bring to the boil; cook, covered, for 4 minutes or until sauce thickens. Season to taste.

2 Cook pasta in a large saucepan of salted boiling water following packet directions until tender; drain. Return pasta to pan.

3 Divide spaghetti and lentil 'bolognese' among plates or bowls; season to taste. Serve topped with pecorino and extra basil leaves.

serving suggestion Serve with garlic bagels (see page 26) and a green salad.

SPAGHETTI BOLOGNESE, CIRCA 1952

The Australian Women's Weekly magazine first published a recipe for 'spaghetti bolognaise' in July 1952, as part of a feature on party suppers. It has since become a staple of Australian dinner tables, with a 2012 Meat and Livestock Australia survey finding 94% of respondents cooked it often or sometimes. To give this recipe a vegetarian update, we used canned lentils instead of beef mince.

TUNA & CHILLI PASTA
WITH DUKKAH CRUMBS

PREP + COOK TIME 35 MINUTES **SERVES** 4

- 500g (1lb) linguine pasta
- 2½ cups (175g) coarsely torn sourdough bread
- ½ cup (125ml) olive oil
- 1 medium red onion (170g), chopped finely
- 3 cloves garlic, crushed

- 2 fresh long red chillies, seeded, chopped finely
- 8 drained anchovy fillets, chopped finely
- 425g (13½oz) canned tuna in chilli oil (see tips)
- 120g (4oz) baby rocket (arugula) leaves
- 2 tablespoons pistachio dukkah spice mix

1 Cook pasta in a large saucepan of salted boiling water following packet directions until just tender. Drain, reserving ½ cup (125ml) of the cooking liquid. Return pasta to pan.

2 Meanwhile, blend or process bread until chopped coarsely.

3 Heat 2 tablespoons of the oil in a medium frying pan over medium heat; cook onion, stirring, for 5 minutes or until softened. Add garlic, chilli and anchovy; cook, stirring, for 1 minute or until fragrant. Add chilli mixture to pasta with tuna, rocket and reserved cooking liquid; toss to combine.

4 Heat 2 tablespoons of the remaining oil in same frying pan over medium heat. Add breadcrumbs; cook, stirring, for 5 minutes or until golden and crisp. Stir in dukkah.

5 Serve pasta mixture sprinkled with dukkah breadcrumbs and drizzled with remaining oil.

tips il you prefer it less spicy, omit the fresh chilli and use regular canned tuna in oil. Serve pasta sprinkled with chopped toasted pine nuts or pistachios, if you like.

FAST BEEF BURGUNDY *WITH PASTA*

PREP + COOK TIME 40 MINUTES **SERVES** 4

- 2 tablespoons ghee (clarified butter) (see tip)
- 600g (1¼lb) beef eye-fillet or rump steak, trimmed, cut into 3cm (1¼in) pieces
- 100g (3oz) streaky bacon, chopped
- 300g (9½oz) small swiss brown mushrooms
- 2 cloves garlic, sliced thinly
- 2 teaspoons fresh thyme leaves, plus extra to serve
- 2 tablespoons tomato paste
- 1 tablespoon plain (all-purpose) flour
- ½ cup (125ml) red wine
- 1 cup (250ml) beef stock
- 300g (9½oz) small pasta shells

1 Heat 2 teaspoons of the ghee in a large, deep, heavy-based frying pan over medium-high heat. Add half the beef; cook, stirring occasionally, for 4 minutes or until browned on all sides. Transfer beef to a plate. Repeat with another 2 teaspoons of ghee and remaining beef; transfer to plate.

2 Heat remaining ghee in same pan; cook bacon and mushrooms, stirring, over medium heat for 3 minutes. Add garlic; cook for 1 minute. Add thyme and tomato paste; cook for 1 minute. Add flour; cook, stirring, for a further 2 minutes.

3 Add wine, bring to the boil over high heat; cook, stirring and scraping base of pan, for 2 minutes or until wine is reduced by half. Add stock, bring to the boil; boil for 2 minutes. Reduce heat to low, return beef to pan; simmer for 4 minutes or until sauce is thickened and beef is tender.

4 Meanwhile cook pasta in a large saucepan of salted boiling water following packet directions until just tender. Drain, reserving ¼ cup (60ml) of the cooking liquid.

5 Add pasta to beef mixture; stir in a little of the reserved pasta water if necessary for sauce to coat pasta. Serve topped with extra thyme leaves.

tip If you don't have ghee, use the same amount of unsalted butter or olive oil.

LOADED VEG MAC 'N' CHEESE

PREP + COOK TIME 45 MINUTES **SERVES** 4

- 375g (12oz) cauliflower, trimmed, cut into large florets
- 1 tablespoon olive oil
- 250g (8oz) macaroni pasta
- 1 cup (240g) light sour cream
- 1¼ cups (310ml) buttermilk
- ½ teaspoon ground nutmeg
- 1 cup (120g) frozen peas
- 2 teaspoons finely grated lemon rind
- 120g (4oz) baby spinach leaves
- 2½ cups (250g) coarsely grated cheddar or pizza cheese
- ¼ cup (60g) finely grated parmesan
- ½ cup (35g) panko (japanese) breadcrumbs
- 1 tablespoon fresh thyme leaves, plus extra to serve

1 Preheat oven to 240°C/475°F. Oil four 2¼ cup (560ml) ovenproof dishes.

2 Place cauliflower on a large oven tray, drizzle with oil and season; toss to coat well. Roast for 15 minutes or until almost tender and browned. Reduce oven to 220°C/425°F.

3 Meanwhile, cook pasta in a large saucepan of salted boiling water following packet directions until tender; drain (see tips).

4 Heat sour cream and buttermilk in a large heavy-based saucepan over low heat. Stir in nutmeg, peas, half the rind, the spinach and three-quarters of the combined cheeses; stir until well combined. Season.

5 Add remaining combined cheeses and rind to breadcrumbs and thyme in a small bowl; stir to combine.

6 Stir pasta into hot cheese sauce; spoon evenly into dishes. Press cauliflower pieces into pasta mixture. Sprinkle evenly with breadcrumb mixture.

7 Bake for 20 minutes or until crumbs are browned and mixture is heated through. Serve topped with extra thyme, if you like.

tips Use a 2.5 litre (10-cup) capacity ovenproof dish, if you prefer. Cook the pasta in boiling water for 2 minutes less than recommended on the packet directions so it will still be quite firm. The pasta will be perfectly cooked after baking. Omit the cauliflower and replace it with roasted pumpkin wedges instead or stir 2 cups (320g) shredded cooked chicken or drained canned tuna in oil into the pasta mixture before baking.

serving suggestion Serve with a green leafy salad.

15

MACARONI CHEESE, CIRCA 1988

The American comfort food, this pasta dish has also had a long history in Australian homes, featuring two of our most beloved foods – pasta and cheese. To give this recipe an update we used light sour cream and buttermilk instead of the heavier, traditional béchamel sauce, and added a healthy dose of green veg.

LINGUINE WITH GARLIC PRAWNS & CHORIZO

PREP + COOK TIME 25 MINUTES **SERVES** 4

- 400g (12½oz) linguine pasta
- 2 tablespoons extra virgin olive oil
- 250g (8oz) cured chorizo sausages, sliced thinly
- 500g (1lb) uncooked large prawns (shrimp), peeled and deveined, tails intact
- 4 cloves garlic, crushed
- 1 fresh long red chilli, seeded, chopped finely
- 1 teaspoon smoked paprika
- 250g (8oz) mixed cherry tomatoes, halved
- 2 teaspoons finely grated lemon rind
- ⅓ cup (80ml) lemon juice
- ⅓ cup finely chopped fresh flat-leaf parsley
- lemon cheeks, to serve

1 Cook pasta in a large saucepan of salted boiling water following packet directions until just tender. Drain, reserving 1 cup (250ml) of the cooking liquid.

2 Meanwhile, heat 2 teaspoons of the oil in a large heavy-based frying pan over medium heat. Cook chorizo, turning, for 3 minutes or until browned; transfer to a plate.

3 Add prawns, garlic, chilli, paprika and tomatoes to pan; cook, stirring occasionally, for 5 minutes or until prawns are just cooked through. Season to taste.

4 Return chorizo to pan; add lemon rind, juice, pasta, parsley and remaining oil. Season. Add enough of the reserved pasta water to coat pasta; toss to coat.

5 Divide pasta mixture among bowls or plates; serve with lemon cheeks. Sprinkle with small flat-leaf parsley leaves, if you like.

PENNE WITH ROASTED PUMPKIN,
ASPARAGUS & PEPITA PESTO

PREP + COOK TIME 40 MINUTES **SERVES** 4

- **800g (1½lb) kent pumpkin, cut into thin wedges**
- **2 tablespoons extra virgin olive oil**
- **340g (11oz) asparagus, cut into 4cm (1½in) lengths**
- **375g (12oz) penne rigate pasta**
- **60g (2oz) baby spinach leaves**
- **120g (4oz) soft goat's cheese, crumbled**
- **1 tablespoon pepitas (pumpkin seed kernels), toasted**

PEPITA PESTO

- **⅓ cup (65g) pepitas (pumpkin seed kernels), toasted**
- **1 clove garlic, crushed**
- **60g (2oz) baby spinach leaves**
- **¼ cup (20g) finely grated parmesan**
- **¼ cup (60ml) extra virgin olive oil**

1 Preheat oven to 200°C/400°F. Line an oven tray with baking paper.

2 Place pumpkin on tray; drizzle with half the oil. Bake for 15 minutes. Add asparagus to tray; roast for a further 5 minutes or until vegetables are just tender.

3 Meanwhile, make pepita pesto.

4 Cook pasta in a large saucepan of salted boiling water following packet directions until just tender. Drain, reserving ½ cup (125ml) of the cooking liquid. Return pasta to pan.

5 Add pesto, asparagus and reserved pasta water to pasta; toss to combine.

6 Divide pasta mixture among plates. Top with pumpkin, spinach and cheese. Serve sprinkled with pepitas and drizzled with remaining oil. Season to taste.

PEPITA PESTO Blend or process pepitas, garlic, spinach and parmesan until coarsely chopped. With motor operating, add oil in a thin, steady stream until combined. Season to taste. Cover surface directly with plastic wrap until required.

tips If you are short of time, use your favourite store-bought pesto instead of making your own. Sprinkle with micro herbs before serving, if you like.

do ahead Pesto can be made up to 3 days ahead; cover the surface directly with plastic wrap to prevent it discolouring and store in the fridge.

FAST LAMB & ROSEMARY RAGOUT
WITH ORECCHIETTE

PREP + COOK TIME 40 MINUTES **SERVES** 6

- 2 tablespoons olive oil
- 500g (1lb) lamb leg steaks or backstraps (eye of loin), cut into 1.5cm (¾in) pieces
- 1 medium onion (150g), chopped finely
- 1 small carrot (70g), grated coarsely
- 3 cloves garlic, chopped finely
- 4 anchovy fillets, chopped finely (see tip)
- 1 tablespoon finely chopped fresh rosemary
- ¼ cup (60ml) balsamic vinegar
- 2 tablespoons tomato paste
- 800g (1½lb) canned diced tomatoes
- 2 teaspoons brown sugar
- 250g (8oz) frozen broad (fava) beans, thawed, peeled
- 500g (1lb) orecchiette pasta
- ½ cup (40g) finely grated parmesan
- ¼ cup fresh basil leaves

1 Heat 1 tablespoon of the oil in a large heavy-based saucepan over high heat; cook lamb, in batches, for 5 minutes or until browned. Transfer to a bowl; cover to keep warm.

2 Heat another 1 tablespoon of the oil in same pan. Add onion, carrot, garlic, anchovy and rosemary; cook, stirring, for 5 minutes or until onion and carrot soften. Add vinegar; cook, stirring, for 30 seconds or until evaporated. Add tomato paste; cook, stirring, for 1 minute or until fragrant.

3 Return lamb to pan with tomatoes and sugar, season; bring to the boil. Reduce heat to low; cook, covered, for 10 minutes. Add broad beans for last 5 minutes of cooking time.

4 Meanwhile, cook pasta in a large saucepan of boiling salted water following packet directions until just tender. Drain, reserving ¼ cup (60ml) of the cooking liquid.

5 Add pasta and reserved pasta water to lamb ragout; stir over medium heat until combined. Season. Serve topped with parmesan and basil leaves.

tip You can omit the anchovies, if preferred.

CHICKEN PAPRIKASH *WITH EGG NOODLES*

PREP + COOK TIME 40 MINUTES **SERVES** 4

- **4 chicken marylands (1.4kg)**
- **2 teaspoons vegetable oil**
- **1 medium onion (150g), sliced thinly**
- **2 cloves garlic, sliced thinly**
- **1 tablespoon sweet paprika**
- **1 tablespoon smoked paprika**
- **2 tablespoons plain (all-purpose) flour**
- **2 cups (500ml) chicken stock**
- **400g (12½oz) canned cherry tomatoes**
- **375g (12oz) fresh egg pasta**

1 Cut end off chicken legs with a sharp cleaver (or ask your butcher to do this). Score skin-side of chicken pieces three times on the diagonal.

2 Heat oil in a large flameproof casserole dish over medium-high heat. Cook chicken, skin-side down, for 5 minutes or until golden brown. Turn chicken; cook for a further 5 minutes. Transfer to a plate.

3 Discard all but 1 tablespoon of fat from pan; reduce heat to medium. Add onion; cook, stirring, for 2 minutes. Add garlic; cook for 2 minutes. Add both paprikas and flour, season; cook, stirring continuously, for 1 minute or until paprika is fragrant.

4 Add stock; whisk until smooth. Add tomatoes; bring to the boil over high heat. Return chicken to pan, skin-side up, in a single layer. Reduce heat to low-medium; cook, covered, stirring occasionally, for 25 minutes or until chicken is cooked through. Season to taste.

5 Meanwhile, cook pasta in a large saucepan of boiling salted water following packet directions until just tender; drain.

6 Serve pasta and chicken paprikash sprinkled with micro herbs, if you like.

tip You could also use 4 thighs and 4 drumsticks, or all drumsticks, or thighs or a whole chicken cut into 4 joints instead of marylands, if you prefer.

serving suggestion Serve with steamed green beans.

CREAMY BEEF & MUSHROOM PASTA
WITH KALE CHIPS

PREP + COOK TIME 30 MINUTES **SERVES** 6

- **500g (1lb) rigatoni pasta**
- **600g (1¼lb) beef fillet steak, sliced thinly**
- **¼ cup (35g) plain (all-purpose) flour**
- **2 tablespoons olive oil**
- **20g (¾oz) butter**
- **1 medium onion (150g), sliced thinly**
- **2 cloves garlic, crushed**
- **375g (12oz) button mushrooms, quartered**
- **⅓ cup (80ml) brandy**
- **2 cups (500ml) beef stock**
- **1 cup (240g) light sour cream**
- **¼ cup finely chopped fresh flat-leaf parsley**
- **¼ cup (20g) finely grated parmesan**

KALE CHIPS
- **200g (6½oz) green kale, washed, dried**
- **1 clove garlic, crushed**
- **2 tablespoons olive oil**

1 Make kale chips.

2 Cook pasta in a large saucepan of salted boiling water following packet directions until tender; drain.

3 Meanwhile, coat beef in flour; shake off excess. Heat oil in a large saucepan over high heat; cook beef, in batches, until browned. Remove from pan; cover to keep warm.

4 Melt butter in same pan; cook onion, garlic and mushrooms, stirring occasionally, until softened. Add brandy; cook, stirring, for 30 seconds. Add stock; bring to the boil. Reduce heat to low; cook for 5 minutes. Add beef and sour cream; stir until smooth. Remove from heat; season. Add parsley; stir until combined.

5 Serve pasta topped with beef mixture, parmesan and kale chips.

KALE CHIPS Preheat oven to 220°C/425°F. Line two large oven trays with baking paper. Tear leafy part of kale from stalks; tear into 3cm (1½in) pieces. Discard stalks. Divide evenly between lined trays. Combine garlic and oil, drizzle half over each tray of kale; toss well to coat. Spread kale out in a single layer. Roat, turning kale and swapping trays from top to bottom shelves of oven halfway through cooking time, for 8 minutes or until kale is crisp.

tips To save time, ask the butcher to slice the beef for you or buy beef stir-fry strips. This recipe is not suitable to freeze.

BEEF STROGANOFF, CIRCA 1988

FOR MANY HOUSEHOLDS, BEEF STROGANOFF IS A UBIQUITOUS WEEKNIGHT DINNER. RICH AND HEARTY, IT'S ALWAYS A WELCOME DISH AT THE DINING TABLE. TO GIVE THIS RECIPE AN UPDATE WE REDUCED THE AMOUNT OF BUTTER AND USED LIGHT SOUR CREAM INSTEAD OF REGULAR CREAM, THEN TOPPED IT OFF WITH CRISPY, MOREISH KALE CHIPS.

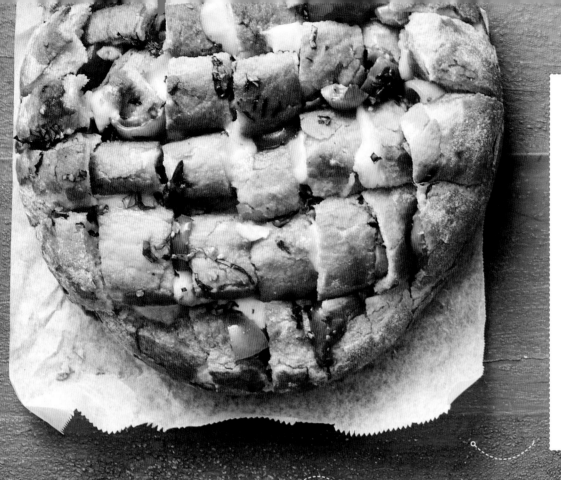

PIZZA LOAF

PREP + COOK TIME
25 MINUTES **SERVES** 6

Preheat oven to 180°C/350°F. Using a serrated knife, cut 1 cobb loaf (400g), 4cm (1½in) apart, three-quarters of the way through; repeat in the other direction to form a cross-hatch pattern. Place on a baking-paper-lined oven tray. Using your hands, crush 250g (8oz) chopped cherry tomatoes in a small bowl. Stir in ⅓ cup chopped pitted sicilian green olives, 2 tablespoons chopped fresh basil, 2 crushed cloves garlic and ¼ cup olive oil; season. Divide tomato mixture and 1 cup coarsely grated mozzarella evenly into each cut. Bake for 15 minutes or until cheese is melted and bread is golden and crisp.
tip For meat-lovers, add salami, ham or pepperoni (or all three).

GARLIC BAGELS

PREP + COOK TIME
25 MINUTES **SERVES** 4

Preheat oven to 200°C/400°F. Combine 100g (3oz) softened butter, 2 tablespoons coarsely chopped fresh flat-leaf parsley and 4 crushed cloves garlic in a small bowl; season. Spread cut sides of 4 halved bagels evenly with butter mixture. Place bagel halves in a single layer, cut-side up, on a baking-paper-lined oven tray. Bake for 20 minutes or until golden and crisp.
tip You can use individual subs or a bread stick cut into lengths, instead of bagels, if you prefer.

GARLIC BREAD

BAGUETTE MONSIEUR

PREP + COOK TIME
30 MINUTES **SERVES** 6

Preheat oven to 180°C/350°F. Cut 1 long baguette (300g), at 2cm (¾in) intervals three-quarters of the way through. Place on a baking-paper-lined oven tray. Combine 100g (3oz) softened butter, 4 crushed cloves garlic, 2 tablespoons dijon mustard and 1 tablespoon fresh thyme leaves in a small bowl; season. Evenly spread butter mixture, 150g (4½oz) thinly sliced ham and 1 cup coarsely grated gruyère cheese in each cut. Bake for 20 minutes or until cheese is melted and bread is golden and crisp.

tip You can use bacon or prosciutto instead ham, if you prefer.

HALOUMI, HERB & GARLIC NAAN

PREP + COOK TIME
25 MINUTES **SERVES** 6

Preheat oven to 180°C/350°F. Place 4 plain naan breads (280g) on a baking-paper-lined oven tray; prick all over with a fork. Combine ⅓ cup extra virgin olive oil, 2 crushed cloves garlic, 2 tablespoons each coarsely chopped fresh flat-leaf parsley and chives and 1 tablespoon coarsely chopped fresh rosemary in a small bowl; season. Spread herb and garlic mixture evenly on bread; top evenly with 125g (4oz) haloumi. Bake for 15 minutes or until bread is golden and crisp.

tip You can use afghan bread instead of naan bread.

THERE IS NOTHING BETTER TO ACCOMPANY A WARM BOWL OF PASTA THAN AN AROMATIC, BUTTERY PIECE OF GARLIC BREAD. OUR 4 VARIATIONS ON THE CLASSIC BRING NEW FLAVOURS WHILE MAINTAINING EVERYTHING THAT MAKES GARLIC BREAD SO SIMPLE & DELICIOUS.

SPAGHETTI WITH LEBANESE-SPICED
LAMB & PINE NUTS

PREP + COOK TIME 50 MINUTES **SERVES** 6

- 2 tablespoons olive oil
- 1 medium onion (150g), chopped finely
- 800g (1½lb) minced (ground) lamb
- 2 cloves garlic, crushed
- 1 teaspoon ground sumac
- 1 tablespoon ground allspice
- 1 teaspoon mixed spice

- ¼ cup (70g) tomato paste
- 400g (12½oz) canned cherry tomatoes
- 500g (1lb) wholemeal spaghetti
- 4 medium ripe tomatoes (640g), chopped finely
- 1 teaspoon finely grated lemon rind
- ½ cup (140g) Greek-style yoghurt
- ⅓ cup (50g) pine nuts, toasted

1   Heat oil in a large heavy-based saucepan over high heat. Cook onion, stirring, for 5 minutes or until softened and browned lightly. Add lamb, stirring with a wooden spoon or fork to break up any clumps. Cook mixture, stirring occasionally, for 8 minutes or until lamb is browned lightly. Discard excess liquid; continue to cook for 5 minutes or until lamb is browned and moisture evaporates.

2   Stir in garlic, spices and tomato paste; cook for a further 3 minutes or until fragrant. Add canned tomatoes, bring to a simmer. Reduce heat to low; cook, covered, for 15 minutes or until sauce is thickened and lamb is tender.

3   Meanwhile, cook spaghetti in a large saucepan of boiling salted water following packet directions until tender. Drain, reserving ¼ cup (60ml) cooking liquid.

4   Stir chopped tomato and rind into lamb mixture; season. Stir spaghetti into lamb mixture; reduce heat to low. Add enough of reserved pasta water to loosen and create a thick sauce; stir well until some of the water is absorbed.

5   Divide pasta mixture among plates; serve topped with yoghurt and pine nuts. Season with pepper.

tips You can use minced beef instead of lamb, if preferred. Sprinkle with small fresh flat-leaf parsley leaves and serve with lemon wedges, if you like.

do ahead Cook the lamb until end of step 2 the day before and refrigerate in an airtight container; reheat just before serving.

serving suggestion Serve with a leafy green salad.

PASTA WITH SMOKY PORK,
CAPSICUM & ROCKET

PREP + COOK TIME 40 MINUTES **SERVES** 4

- **600g (1½lb) pork fillets, cut into 1.5cm (¾in) dice (see tips)**
- **2 tablespoons olive oil**
- **1 large red onion (300g), chopped finely**
- **2 medium red capsicums (bell peppers) (400g), cut into thin strips**
- **1 tablespoon chopped fresh rosemary**
- **500g (1lb) large pasta shells**
- **120g (4oz) wild rocket (arugula)**

SMOKY CAPSICUM PASTE
- **270g (8½oz) jar roasted capsicum, drained**
- **3 teaspoons smoked paprika**
- **2 cloves garlic, peeled**
- **¼ cup (60ml) extra virgin olive oil**

1 Make smoky capsicum paste.

2 Add pork to capsicum paste; stir to coat well.

3 Heat oil in a large heavy-based frying pan over medium heat. Add onion and capsicum; cook, stirring, for 5 minutes or until softened.

4 Increase heat to high, add rosemary and pork mixture; stir to combine. Cook, covered, for 10 minutes or until pork is tender and sauce is thickened.

5 Meanwhile, cook pasta in a large saucepan of salted boiling water following packet directions until just tender. Drain, reserving ¼ cup (60ml) cooking liquid. Add pasta to pork mixture with enough of reserved pasta water to form a thick sauce; stir to mix well. Season; stir through half the rocket.

6 Serve pasta mixture topped with remaining rocket and extra rosemary, if you like.

SMOKY CAPSICUM PASTE Process or blend ingredients until a smooth puree forms. Transfer to a medium bowl. (Makes 1 cup)

tips Cut the pork into small pieces so it cooks quickly and is easy to eat. Instead of making your own smoky capsicum paste, use a purchased Balkan red capsicum paste, called ajvar, available in jars from some major supermarkets and delicatessens.

do ahead Make the smoky capsicum paste up to 3 days ahead; store in an airtight container in the fridge.

veg instead To make this vegetarian, omit the pork and add a drained, rinsed 400g (12½oz) can cannellini beans in step 3. Stir the capsicum paste through the cooked pasta in step 5 and sprinkle with 200g (6½oz) crumbled fetta before serving.

SPRING VEGETABLE PASTA
WITH MINTY PEA PESTO

PREP + COOK TIME 35 MINUTES **SERVES** 4

- 375g (12oz) fresh pappardelle pasta
- 2 tablespoons olive oil
- 2 cloves garlic, crushed
- 250g (8oz) frozen broad (fava) beans, thawed, peeled
- 200g (6½oz) asparagus, halved lengthways
- 2 small zucchini (180g), peeled into ribbons
- 120g (4oz) yellow beans, halved on the diagonal
- 2 medium lemons (280g), rind finely grated, juice squeezed
- 100g (3oz) fresh ricotta
- 40g (1½oz) pecorino cheese, grated finely
- ¼ cup fresh mint leaves

MINTY PEA PESTO
- 2 cups (240g) frozen peas, thawed
- 1 cup fresh mint leaves
- ¼ cup (35g) roasted unsalted shelled pistachios
- 1 clove garlic, crushed
- ⅓ cup (80ml) extra virgin olive oil
- ½ cup (40g) pecorino cheese, grated finely

1 Make minty pea pesto.

2 Cook pasta in a large saucepan of salted boiling water following packet directions. Drain, reserving ½ cup of the cooking liquid.

3 Meanwhile, heat oil in a large heavy-based frying pan over low heat; cook garlic for 1 minute or until fragrant. Increase heat to high, add all vegetables; cook for 2 minutes or until vegetables begin to soften but are still vibrant.

4 Stir pesto into vegetable mixture. Add pasta, lemon juice and enough of the reserved pasta water to loosen and coat pasta mixture. Stir gently over medium heat for 2 minutes or until sauce is thickened and combined; season to taste.

5 Serve pasta mixture topped with ricotta, pecorino, lemon rind and mint.

MINTY PEA PESTO Process peas, mint, pistachios, garlic and oil in a small food processor until smooth. Transfer to a small bowl, stir through pecorino; season to taste.

tips Instead of zucchini and yellow beans, you can use your favourite fresh spring vegetables instead – try sugar snap peas, snow peas or green beans. Top with snow pea sprouts before serving, if you like.

CHICKEN SALTIMBOCCA *TORTELLINI*

PREP + COOK TIME 35 MINUTES **SERVES** 4

- **8 slices prosciutto (120g)**
- **340g (11oz) cheese tortellini**
- **50g (1½oz) butter**
- **1 medium leek (350g), sliced thinly**
- **200g (6½oz) swiss brown mushrooms, sliced**
- **2 cloves garlic, crushed**
- **600g (1¼lb) chicken tenderloins, cut into 2.5cm (1in) pieces**
- **½ cup (125ml) dry white wine**
- **½ bunch fresh sage, shredded, plus extra small leaves, to serve**
- **300ml thickened (heavy) cream**
- **2 medium zucchini (240g), diced finely**
- **1 medium lemon (140g)**
- **2 tablespoons freshly grated parmesan**
- **lemon wedges, to serve**

1 Preheat grill (broiler) to high. Line an oven tray with baking paper.

2 Place prosciutto on lined tray; grill for 1 minute on each side or until crisp.

3 Cook tortellini in a large saucepan of salted boiling water following packet directions until just tender. Drain; return to pan to keep warm.

4 Meanwhile, melt butter in a large deep frying pan over medium heat; cook leek and mushrooms, stirring, for 5 minutes or until softened and browned lightly.

5 Add garlic and chicken; cook, stirring occasionally, for 3 minutes or until browned. Add wine; cook for 1 minute or until almost evaporated. Add sage, cream and zucchini, bring to the boil over high heat; cook for 2 minutes or until chicken is cooked through.

6 Using a zesting tool, remove rind from lemon into long strips; juice lemon. Add chicken mixture and lemon juice to pasta, season to taste; toss to combine.

7 Top pasta mixture with torn prosciutto, lemon rind, parmesan and extra sage leaves. Serve with lemon wedges.

tip You can use 500g fresh fettuccine instead of the tortellini, if you like.

BAKED CHICKEN, PEA & RICOTTA MEATBALLS
WITH SPAGHETTI

PREP + COOK TIME 50 MINUTES **SERVES** 4

- ⅔ cup (80g) frozen peas
- 2 cups (500ml) boiling water
- 2 teaspoons finely grated lemon rind
- ¼ cup coarsely chopped fresh mint
- 350g (11oz) minced (ground) chicken
- 2 cloves garlic, crushed
- ¼ cup (25g) dried multigrain breadcrumbs
- 1 egg
- ⅓ cup (80g) fresh ricotta
- 1 tablespoon olive oil
- 800g (1½lb) canned diced tomatoes
- 3 teaspoons balsamic vinegar
- 500g (1lb) spelt spaghetti
- 2 tablespoons finely grated parmesan

1 Preheat oven to 240°C/475°F. Oil and line a shallow roasting pan with baking paper.

2 Place peas in a medium heatproof bowl; cover with the boiling water. Stand peas for 1 minute; drain, reserving 1 tablespoon of the water. Blend or process peas, reserved water, rind and chopped mint until just combined.

3 Combine chicken, garlic, breadcrumbs and egg in a medium bowl; mix well. Stir in pea mixture and ricotta.

4 Using wet hands, roll level tablespoons of mixture into balls. Place in roasting pan; drizzle with oil. Roast meatballs for 15 minutes, turning once. Add tomatoes and vinegar; roast for a further 15 minutes or until meatballs are cooked through and sauce is hot.

5 Meanwhile, cook pasta in a large saucepan of salted boiling water following packet directions until just tender. Drain.

6 Divide pasta, meatballs and sauce among plates; season to taste. Serve topped with parmesan and micro herbs or small fresh mint leaves, if you like.

do ahead You can freeze the raw or cooked meatballs; thaw in the fridge before cooking or reheating.

SUMMER SPAGHETTI *WITH CHICKEN*

PREP + COOK TIME 35 MINUTES (+ COOLING) **SERVES** 4

- **1 litre (4 cups) water**
- **300g (9½oz) chicken breast fillets**
- **375g (12oz) spaghetti rigate**
- **¼ cup (60ml) olive oil**
- **1 clove garlic, crushed**
- **250g (8oz) cherry tomatoes, halved**
- **100g (3oz) cherry bocconcini cheese**
- **80g (2½oz) rocket (arugula)**
- **⅓ cup fresh basil leaves, torn**

ROCKET & LEMON PESTO
- **¼ cup (40g) toasted pine nuts**
- **¼ cup firmly packed fresh small basil leaves**
- **40g (1oz) rocket (arugula)**
- **¼ cup (60ml) lemon juice**
- **¾ cup (60g) finely grated parmesan**
- **¾ cup (180ml) extra virgin olive oil**

1 Bring the water to the boil in a medium saucepan. Add chicken; return to the boil. Reduce heat to low; simmer, partially covered, for 10 minutes or until chicken is just cooked through. Remove chicken from pan; cool for 10 minutes, then shred coarsely.

2 Meanwhile, cook pasta in a large saucepan of salted boiling water following packet directions until tender. Drain, reserving ¼ cup (60ml) cooking liquid. Return pasta to pan.

3 Make rocket and lemon pesto.

4 Reheat pasta over low heat, stirring, until hot. Add 2 tablespoons of reserved pasta water, the pesto, oil, garlic, chicken, tomatoes, bocconcini and rocket; toss gently to combine. Season to taste. Add remaining pasta water, if you prefer.

5 Serve pasta topped with basil.

ROCKET & LEMON PESTO Blend or process all ingredients until almost smooth; season to taste. (Makes 1½ cups)

tip Swap the chicken with a drained 425g (13½oz) can of tuna in oil or 500g (1lb) peeled cooked king prawns, if you like.

veg instead To make this vegetarian, omit the poached chicken and use a vegetarian parmesan in the pesto.

WARM MINESTRONE PASTA SALAD

PREP + COOK TIME 45 MINUTES **SERVES** 4

- **375g (12oz) fusilli pasta**
- **olive oil spray**
- **2 small zucchini (180g), sliced thinly**
- **400g (12½oz) canned borlotti beans, drained, rinsed**
- **135g (2oz) jar roasted capsicum, sliced thickly (see tips)**
- **200g (6½oz) baby roma tomatoes, halved lengthways**
- **1 small radicchio (150g), trimmed, shredded**
- **½ small red onion (50g), chopped finely**
- **200g (6½oz) cherry bocconcini, torn**
- **½ cup fresh basil leaves**

SEMI-DRIED TOMATO PESTO

- **½ cup (75g) drained coarsely chopped semi-dried tomatoes, plus ¼ cup (60ml) reserved oil**
- **1½ tablespoons pine nuts, toasted**
- **1½ tablespoons freshly grated parmesan**
- **1 tablespoon balsamic vinegar**
- **1 clove garlic, crushed**
- **1 teaspoon dried oregano**
- **1 teaspoon dried basil**

1 Make semi-dried tomato pesto.

2 Cook pasta in a large saucepan of salted boiling water following packet directions until tender. Drain, reserving ¼ cup (60ml) cooking liquid. Return pasta to pan. Cool slightly.

3 Meanwhile, heat an oiled grill pan (or plate) over medium-high heat. Spray zucchini with oil; cook, for 2 minutes on each side or until tender and char marks appear.

4 Add pesto, borlotti beans, capsicum and zucchini to pasta; cook, stirring gently, over medium heat for 3 minutes or until warmed through and well combined. Stir in a little of the reserved pasta water if necessary to loosen the sauce; remove from heat. Add tomatoes, radicchio, onion and bocconcini; toss gently to combine.

5 Transfer pasta mixture to a platter; sprinkle with basil leaves. Season to taste.

SEMI-DRIED TOMATO PESTO Process tomatoes, pine nuts, parmesan, vinegar, garlic, oregano and basil until a chunky paste forms. With motor operating, add reserved oil in a steady stream and process until combined; you may need to add a little more olive oil. Season to taste. (Makes 1 cup)

tips If you are short of time, use 1 cup of your favourite store-bought pesto instead of making your own. You will need half a 270g (4oz) jar roasted capsicum for this recipe. Add 150g (4½oz) bacon, if you like; grill it in step 3 for 5 minutes before adding the zucchini. Use drained sun-dried tomatoes in oil instead of semi-dried tomatoes, if you prefer.

MINESTRONE WITH MEATBALLS, CIRCA 1992

To give this recipe an update we have transformed what can sometimes be a stodgy, lacklustre soup into a summery salad, studded with fresh tomatoes and herbs. The bold flavours of the pesto reflect the tomato base of the soup, while bringing punchy notes to the pasta with the inclusion of the balsamic vinegar.

BREAKFAST-FOR-DINNER PASTA

PREP + COOK TIME 30 MINUTES **SERVES** 4

- 400g (12½oz) orecchiette pasta
- 2 tablespoons olive oil
- 3 fresh chorizo sausages (270g), skin peeled, broken into 2cm (¾in) pieces
- 1 large red onion (300g), cut into thin wedges
- 150g (4½oz) cavolo nero (tuscan cabbage), stems discarded, leaves shredded finely

- 4 eggs
- 4 slices prosciutto (60g)
- 250g (8oz) truss cherry tomatoes, cut into clusters
- 1 cup (240g) fresh ricotta
- ⅔ cup (50g) finely grated parmesan
- ¼ cup small flat-leaf parsley leaves

1 Cook pasta in a large saucepan of boiling salted water following packet directions until just tender. Drain, reserving ⅓ cup (80ml) cooking liquid.

2 Meanwhile, heat oil in a large heavy-based frying pan over medium heat. Add chorizo and onion; cook, stirring, for 5 minutes or until golden. Add cavolo nero; cook for 4 minutes or until softened. Add reserved pasta water; season to taste.

3 Half-fill a large frying pan with water; bring to the boil. Break one egg into a cup, then slide into pan; repeat with remaining eggs. When all eggs are in pan, return water to the boil. Cover pan, turn off heat; stand for 4 minutes or until a light film of egg white sets over yolks. Remove eggs, one at a time, using a slotted spoon; place spoon on paper-towel-lined saucer to blot up any poaching liquid.

4 Preheat grill (broiler) to high. Line an oven tray with baking paper. Place prosciutto and tomatoes on tray; grill for 2 minutes or until prosciutto is crisp and tomatoes soften.

5 Combine pasta, chorizo mixture and crumbled ricotta; divide among plates. Serve topped evenly with eggs, prosciutto, tomatoes, parmesan and parsley, season with pepper.

tips Cavolo nero is a type of kale; if unavailable, use regular kale instead. If you can't find truss cherry tomatoes, use regular cherry or grape tomatoes instead.

CORIANDER BEEF

GARLIC

CHILLI NOODLES

MUSHROOMS

BROCCOLINI

SHALLOTS

CHICKEN

LIMES SESAME

SALT & PEPPER

& GINGER HONEY

STIR-FRIES

BROWN RICE NASI GORENG

PREP + COOK TIME 45 MINUTES **SERVES** 4

- 400g (12½oz) gai lan
- 375g (12oz) choy sum
- ½ cup fresh coriander (cilantro) leaves
- ¼ cup (60ml) peanut oil
- 4 eggs
- 6 shallots (150g), halved, sliced thinly
- 4cm (1½in) piece fresh ginger (20g), cut into thin matchsticks
- 2 cloves garlic, crushed
- 1 fresh long red chilli, sliced thinly
- 150g (4½oz) button mushrooms, sliced
- 100g (3oz) shiitake mushrooms, sliced thinly
- 115g (3½oz) baby corn
- 3½ cups (625g) cooked brown rice (see tips)
- 2 tablespoons kecap manis
- 1 teaspoon sesame oil
- lime wedges, to serve

1 Cut stalks from gai lan and choy sum. Cut stalks into 10cm (4in) lengths; cut leaves into 10cm (4in) pieces. Keep stalks and leaves separated. Coarsely chop half the coriander; reserve remaining whole leaves.

2 Heat 2 teaspoons of the peanut oil a non-stick frying pan over medium–high heat. Add eggs; cook for 2 minutes or until the whites are firm, edges are crisp and the yolks are cooked to your liking.

3 Heat 2 tablespoons of the peanut oil in a wok over medium heat; stir-fry shallots for 8 minutes or until soft and light golden. Add ginger, garlic and half the chilli; stir-fry for 4 minutes or until softened. Transfer shallot mixture to a plate.

4 Heat remaining peanut oil in wok over medium–high heat; stir-fry mushrooms and corn for 4 minutes or until just tender. Add gai lan and choy sum stalks; stir-fry for 3 minutes. Add gai lan and choy sum leaves, cooked rice, kecap manis, sesame oil, shallot mixture and chopped coriander; stir-fry 3 minutes or until rice is hot and leaves are wilted. Season.

5 Top nasi goreng with fried eggs, reserved coriander leaves and remaining chilli. Serve with lime wedges.

tips You will need to cook 1½ cups (300g) brown rice for the amount of cooked rice needed in this recipe. Use any leafy green vegetables you like in this vegetarian take on Indonesia-style fried rice.

do ahead You can cook the rice a day in advance and refrigerate in an airtight container, if you like.

FRIED RICE, CIRCA 1985

AUSTRALIANS HAVE LOVED ASIAN FOOD FOR DECADES, BUT LACKING THE AUTHENTIC INGREDIENTS AND THE TASTE FOR SOME OF ITS MORE SPICY ELEMENTS, THE RESULTS WERE OFTEN FAR FROM THE ORIGINAL. TO GIVE THIS RECIPE AN UPDATE WE HAVE SWAPPED REGULAR WHITE RICE WITH ITS MORE WHOLESOME COUNTERPART, BROWN RICE, AND BID THE PEAS FAREWELL IN FAVOUR OF A MEGA DOSE OF VITAMIN-RICH LEAFY ASIAN GREENS.

CHEAT'S MUSHU PORK

PREP + COOK TIME 35 MINUTES (+ REFRIGERATION & COOLING) **SERVES** 4

- 600g (1¼lb) pork leg or loin steaks
- 1½ tablespoons light soy sauce
- 1 teaspoon white (granulated) sugar
- 1 teaspoon sesame oil
- 4 eggs, beaten lightly
- 4 green onions (scallions), sliced thinly
- 2 tablespoons vegetable oil
- 1 tablespoon finely chopped fresh ginger
- 2 cloves garlic, chopped finely
- 1 medium leek (350g), white part only, sliced thinly
- 200g (6½oz) fresh shiitake mushrooms, sliced thinly
- ¼ cup (60ml) chicken stock
- ¼ cup (60ml) hoisin sauce
- 1 teaspoon cornflour (cornstarch)
- 8 small white corn tortillas (200g)
- 1 lebanese cucumber (130g), julienned
- ½ cup (40g) bean sprouts

1 Using a meat mallet or rolling pin, pound pork until 5mm (¼in) thick. Place pork, soy sauce and sugar in a bowl; stir to combine. Cover; refrigerate for 3 hours or overnight.

2 Heat sesame oil in large non-stick frying pan over medium high heat; swirl pan to coat with oil. Add egg; cook for 4 minutes or until omelette starts to set around edge. Sprinkle over half of green onion. Use a spatula to gently drag egg mixture from centre to edge of pan; cook until firm. Slide omelette onto a chopping board. When cool enough to handle, roll omelette into a log; cut into 1cm (½in) thick slices.

3 Heat half the vegetable oil in a wok or large heavy-based frying pan over high heat. Add pork to wok; cook for 2 minutes or until browned and just cooked through. Transfer pork to a plate.

4 Heat remaining vegetable oil in wok over high heat. Add ginger, garlic, leek and remaining green onion; stir-fry for 2 minutes or until leek is tender. Add mushrooms; stir-fry for 2 minutes or until golden and cooked.

5 Slice pork thinly on the diagonal; return pork to wok. Combine stock, hoisin sauce and cornflour in a small bowl; add to wok. Stir to combine; cook for 4 minutes or until sauce boils and coats pork.

6 Meanwhile, warm tortillas following packet directions.

7 Just before serving, divide pork mixture among warm tortillas; top evenly with omelette, cucumber and bean sprouts.

tip Serve topped with sriracha or your favourite chilli sauce and micro herbs, if you like.

STIR-FRIED CHICKEN
WITH TAMARI ALMOND CRUMBLE

PREP + COOK TIME 35 MINUTES (+ STANDING & COOLING) **SERVES** 4

- 2 tablespoons light soy sauce
- 1 tablespoon chinese cooking wine (shao hsing)
- 1 teaspoon sea salt flakes
- 1 teaspoon white (granulated) sugar
- 600g (1¼lb) chicken breast fillets, sliced thickly on the diagonal
- ¼ cup (60ml) vegetable oil
- 4 trimmed celery stalks (400g), cut into 4cm (1½in) lengths on the diagonal
- 2 fresh long red chillies, sliced thinly
- 200g (6½oz) snow peas, halved lengthways
- 5cm (2in) piece fresh ginger, peeled, julienned
- 2 cloves garlic, sliced thinly
- 4 green onions (scallions), sliced thinly
- ¼ teaspoon sesame oil

TAMARI ALMOND CRUMBLE

- ¼ cup (40g) tamari almonds
- 1½ tablespoons white sesame seeds
- ¼ cup finely chopped fresh coriander (cilantro)

1 Combine 1 tablespoon of the soy sauce, the cooking wine, salt and sugar in a medium bowl; add chicken. Toss chicken to coat in marinade. Cover; stand for 15 minutes for flavours to develop.

2 Meanwhile, make tamari almond crumble.

3 Heat 1 tablespoon of the vegetable oil in a wok or large heavy-based frying pan over high heat. Add celery and chilli; stir-fry for 3 minutes or until just tender. Stir through 1 tablespoon of the soy sauce; transfer to a large plate.

4 Rinse wok; wipe clean. Heat another 1 tablespoon of the oil in wok over high heat; add chicken, discard marinade. Stir-fry chicken for 8 minutes or until browned and cooked through. Transfer to a bowl.

5 Add remaining oil to wok, add snow peas, ginger, garlic and green onion; stir-fry for 2 minutes or until aromatic. Return chicken to wok with sesame oil; stir to combine.

6 Combine chicken mixture and vegetables, sprinkle with tamari almond crumble.

TAMARI ALMOND CRUMBLE Place almonds and sesame seeds in a dry heavy-based frying pan over medium heat. Cook, shaking pan, for 2 minutes or until sesame seeds are golden. Transfer to a bowl; cool. Process almond mixture until chopped coarsely. Add coriander and pulse until just combined. Transfer to a small bowl.

do ahead You can marinate the chicken in a covered bowl in the fridge for 2 hours or overnight, if you like.

serving suggestion Serve with steamed rice and extra sliced green onion (scallions).

CHICKEN AND ALMONDS, CIRCA 1978

To give this recipe an update we have swapped the blanched almonds in the classic chinese takeaway staple with a crunchy tamari almond crumble, then pumped up the green veg. We have also dialled back the sugar-packed sauce to let the fresh ingredients shine.

LEMON GRASS BEEF NOODLE SALAD

PREP + COOK TIME 35 MINUTES (+ REFRIGERATION) **SERVES** 4

- 600g (1¼lb) beef porterhouse steaks, sliced thinly on the diagonal (see tips)
- 2 tablespoons fish sauce
- 3 stems fresh lemon grass, white part only, chopped finely
- 2 cloves garlic, crushed
- 2 tablespoons vegetable oil
- 1 red shallot (25g), halved, sliced thinly
- 2 teaspoons white (granulated) sugar

VERMICELLI SALAD
- ¼ cup (60ml) fish sauce
- 1½ tablespoons rice wine vinegar
- 1½ tablespoons caster (superfine) sugar
- ¼ cup (60ml) olive oil
- ¼ cup (60ml) lime juice
- 200g (6½oz) dried rice vermicelli noodles
- 1 fresh long red chilli, seeded, sliced thinly
- 3 baby cucumbers (qukes) (180g), sliced thinly on the diagonal (see tips)
- 1 medium carrot (120g), sliced thinly into ribbons with a vegetable peeler (see tips)
- 1 cup fresh mint leaves
- 1 cup fresh vietnamese mint leaves

1 Place beef in a medium bowl with fish sauce and half of each the lemon grass and garlic; stir to mix well. Refrigerate, covered, for at least 30 minutes for flavours to develop.

2 Meanwhile, make vermicelli salad.

3 Heat a wok or large heavy-based frying pan over high heat. Add half the oil; stir-fry half the beef for 3 minutes or until just browned. Transfer to a plate. Repeat with remaining beef.

4 Heat remaining oil in wok. Add shallot and remaining lemon grass and garlic; stir-fry for 2 minutes or until fragrant. Return beef to wok, add sugar; stir-fry for 30 seconds. Season to taste.

5 Divide salad among bowls or plates; top evenly with beef. Drizzle with remaining dressing

VERMICELLI SALAD For the dressing, place fish sauce, vinegar, sugar, oil and lime juice in a screw-top jar; shake well. Place noodles in a bowl, pour boiling water over to cover, stand for 2 minutes to soften. Drain well. Place noodles and remaining ingredients in a large bowl with half the dressing; toss gently to coat.

tips Swap porterhouse steaks with rump steaks, if you prefer. Use 2 lebanese cucumbers if qukes are not available. Cut the carrot into julienne or grate coarsely, if you prefer.

serving suggestion Serve topped with crisp-fried shallots, finely chopped green onion (scallions) and coarsely chopped roasted unsalted peanuts, with trimmed butter lettuce leaves to use as cups.

FAST LAMB & POTATO 'CURRY'
WITH CUCUMBER & MINT PICKLE

PREP + COOK TIME 45 MINUTES (+ REFRIGERATION & STANDING) **SERVES** 4

- 600g (1¼lb) lamb fillets, cut into 2cm (¾in) pieces
- 1 teaspoon ground cumin
- 1 tablespoon light soy sauce
- 1 teaspoon white (granulated) sugar
- 400g (12½oz) baby (new) potatoes, halved if large
- 1 tablespoon vegetable oil
- 3 cloves garlic, sliced thinly
- 5cm (2in) piece fresh ginger, peeled, julienned
- 1 large onion (150g), cut into thin wedges
- ¼ cup (60ml) kecap manis
- ½ cup (125ml) water
- 2 green onions (scallions), sliced thinly
- 1 fresh long red chilli, sliced thinly
- lime wedges, to serve

CUCUMBER & MINT PICKLE

- 6 baby cucumbers (qukes) (180g), sliced thinly with a vegetable peeler
- ½ cup (20g) alfalfa sprouts (see tips)
- 1 tablespoon rice wine vinegar
- 1 tablespoon lime juice
- ½ teaspoon sea salt flakes
- ½ teaspoon white (granulated) sugar
- 1 cup (50g) fresh mint leaves, shredded

1 Place lamb, cumin, soy sauce and sugar in a medium bowl; toss lamb to coat in marinade. Cover with plastic wrap; refrigerate for at least 30 minutes for flavours to develop.

2 Meanwhile, place potatoes in a small saucepan; cover with cold water. Bring to the boil; remove from heat. Stand for 15 minutes in water; drain well.

3 Make cucumber and mint pickle.

4 Heat a wok or large frying pan over high heat. Add oil and lamb mixture; cook, without stirring, for 3 minutes or until lamb is well browned. Shake wok; turn lamb over. Cook lamb for a further 3 minutes without turning; transfer to a bowl.

5 Add garlic, ginger and onion to wok; stir-fry for 1 minute or until fragrant.

6 Stir in kecap manis and the water; bring sauce to the boil over high heat. Reduce heat to medium; simmer for 5 minutes or until sauce is thickened. Add lamb and potatoes; stir gently for 3 minutes or until coated in sauce and warmed through.

7 Top lamb and potato 'curry' with green onion and chilli. Serve with cucumber and mint pickle and lime wedges.

CUCUMBER & MINT PICKLE Place cucumber and sprouts in a medium bowl. Combine vinegar, lime juice, salt and sugar in a small jug. Pour over cucumber mixture; stir to mix. Cover; refrigerate for up to 30 minutes. Stir through mint just before serving.

tips This Indonesian-inspired dry curry is big on flavour without the chilli; chilli lovers could serve this with sambal oelek or their favourite chilli sauce and add finely chopped fresh red chilli to the pickle. Use 1 cup (80g) bean sprouts instead of alfalfa, if preferred. It's important to add the mint to the pickle just before serving, otherwise it will blacken.

serving suggestion Serve with store-bought roti or naan or steamed basmati rice.

STICKY CHICKEN
WITH ZUCCHINI 'NOODLES'

PREP + COOK TIME 15 MINUTES **SERVES** 4

- **600g (1lb) chicken thigh fillets, trimmed, sliced thickly**
- **½ teaspoon chinese five-spice powder**
- **2 teaspoons brown sugar**
- **1 tablespoon sweet chilli sauce**
- **1 tablespoon light soy sauce**
- **5 medium zucchini (500g)**
- **1 tablespoon olive oil**
- **400g (12½oz) gai lan, trimmed, cut into 5cm (2in) lengths**
- **2 tablespoons water**
- **2 green onions (scallions), sliced thinly**
- **1 fresh long red chilli, sliced thinly**
- **2 tablespoons fresh coriander (cilantro) leaves**

1 Combine chicken with spice, sugar and half of each of the sauces in a medium bowl.

2 Using a vegetable spiraliser, cut zucchini into noodles (see tips).

3 Heat a wok over high heat, add oil; stir-fry chicken mixture, in batches, until chicken is browned, cooked through and sticky. Transfer to a bowl. Wipe wok clean.

4 Add gai lan and the water to wok; stir-fry for 1 minute or until gai lan is just tender. Add remaining sauces; stir-fry for 1 minute or until heated through. Add zucchini to wok; toss gently until just combined.

5 Serve noodle mixture topped with chicken and sprinkled with green onion, chilli and coriander leaves.

tips If you have a vegetable spiraliser, making vegetable noodles such as these zucchini ones is a cinch. If not, use a julienne peeler, V-slicer or the coarse side of a box grater instead. Alternatively, swap the zucchini 'noodles' for bean thread vermicelli, hokkien noodles or steamed rice.

do ahead Chicken can be marinated a day ahead; cover and refrigerate.

CHICKEN CHOW MEIN, CIRCA 1978

To give this recipe an update we reduced the carbs by ditching the stodgy noodles, and replacing them with fresh zoodles — 'noodles' made from spiralised zucchini. You can spiralise your favourite veg instead of the zucchini, if you like - carrot or orange sweet potato would work well in this recipe.

BIBIMBAP

PREP + COOK TIME 50 MINUTES (+ REFRIGERATION) **SERVES** 4

- 500g (1lb) rump steak, sliced thinly against the grain
- 1 tablespoon finely grated fresh ginger
- 3 cloves garlic, chopped finely
- 3 green onions (scallions), sliced thinly
- 2 tablespoons mirin
- ¼ cup (60ml) light soy sauce
- 1 tablespoon sesame oil
- 1¼ cups (245g) white long-grain rice
- 1¾ cups (430ml) water
- ¼ cup (60ml) vegetable oil
- 100g (1oz) fresh shiitake mushrooms, trimmed (see tips)
- 4 eggs
- 1 kohlrabi (500g), julienned (see tips)
- 2 cups (160g) finely shredded red cabbage
- 4 baby (dutch) carrots (80g), sliced thinly (see tips)
- 1 medium red capsicum (bell pepper) (200g), julienned
- 100g (3oz) snow pea sprouts
- 1 tablespoon white sesame seeds

SOY-SESAME SAUCE
- 2 teaspoons sesame oil
- 2 teaspoons white sesame seeds, toasted
- 1 teaspoon light soy sauce
- 1 clove garlic, crushed

1 Place beef, ginger, garlic, green onion, mirin, soy sauce and sesame oil in a medium bowl; stir to combine. Cover; refrigerate for 3 hours or overnight.

2 Make soy-sesame sauce.

3 Rinse rice in cold water until water runs clear; drain. Place rice in a medium heavy-based saucepan with the water; bring to the boil. Reduce heat to low; cook, covered, for 12 minutes or until rice is tender and water is absorbed. Leave to stand, covered.

4 Meanwhile, heat a wok or large heavy-based frying pan over high heat. Add 1 tablespoon of the oil; stir-fry mushrooms for 4 minutes or until browned. Transfer to a bowl; stir in half the soy-sesame sauce.

5 Drain beef with a slotted spoon or strainer; reserve marinade. Heat clean wok over high heat; add another 1 tablespoon of oil. Stir-fry half the beef for 5 minutes or until brown; transfer to a bowl. Repeat with another 2 teaspoons oil and remaining beef. Add reserved marinade and remaining soy-sesame sauce to wok; stir-fry for 1 minute or until sauce is reduced. Return beef to wok; stir-fry for 1 minute or until coated in sauce and warmed through.

6 Heat a non-stick frying pan over medium–high heat. Add remaining oil; cook eggs until the whites are firm, edges are crisp and the yolks are cooked to your liking.

7 Divide rice among bowls; top evenly with beef mixture, vegetables and fried eggs. Sprinkle with sesame seeds. Mix ingredients together in bowl before eating.

SOY-SESAME SAUCE Combine ingredients in a small bowl.

tips Use fresh mixed asian mushrooms instead of all shiitake mushrooms and daikon radish or shaved baby radishes instead of kohlrabi, if you like. Use a mandoline or V-slicer, if you have one, to thinly slice the carrots. Swap bean sprouts or alfalfa for snow pea sprouts, if preferred.

do ahead Beef can be marinated a day ahead; cover and refrigerate.

TAMARIND-HONEY PORK & PINEAPPLE
WITH RICE NOODLE SALAD

PREP + COOK TIME 40 MINUTES **SERVES** 4

- 1 tablespoon vegetable oil
- 600g (1¼lb) pork fillet, sliced thickly against the grain
- 3 cloves garlic, crushed
- ⅓ cup (100g) tamarind concentrate (puree)
- 2 tablespoons kecap manis
- 1 tablespoon honey
- ⅓ cup (80ml) water
- ½ small pineapple (450g), cored, sliced thinly
- lime wedges, to serve

RICE NOODLE SALAD
- 100g (3oz) rice vermicelli
- 2 lebanese cucumbers (260g), sliced thinly into ribbons
- 240g truss cherry tomatoes, halved (see tips)
- ½ cup each fresh mint, coriander (cilantro) and thai basil leaves
- 1 tablespoon fish sauce
- 2 tablespoons lime juice
- 2 teaspoons olive oil

1 Make rice noodle salad.

2 Heat a wok over high heat, add oil; stir-fry pork and garlic for 3 minutes on each side or until pork is golden and almost cooked through. Add remaining ingredients, except lime wedges; stir-fry until hot.

3 Serve stir-fry with noodle salad and lime wedges.

RICE NOODLE SALAD Place noodles in a large bowl, pour boiling water over to cover, stand for 2 minutes to soften; drain well. Return to bowl; add cucumber, tomato and herbs. Combine fish sauce, lime juice and oil in a small bowl; add to salad and toss gently to mix. Season to taste.

tips Tamarind adds a tart, sweet and sour flavour to food, which works here in this modern take on the Chinese take-away staple, sweet and sour pork. Tamarind concentrate is available in jars or plastic containers from major supermarkets and asian grocers. Swap chicken breast fillets for the pork, if preferred. We used sweet cherry truss tomatoes, but you could use regular cherry or grape tomatoes, if you like.

SWEET AND SOUR PORK, CIRCA 1984

TO GIVE THIS RECIPE AN UPDATE WE LEFT THE DEEP-FRYER IN THE CUPBOARD IN FAVOUR OF STIR-FRYING THINLY SLICED, LEAN PORK FILLET INSTEAD. THE GLUGGY SWEET AND SOUR SAUCE OF OLD IS REPLACED WITH THE SWEETNESS OF HONEY AND SOURNESS OF TAMARIND, STUDDED WITH CHUNKS OF FRESH, RIPE PINEAPPLE.

STEAMED **GINGER RICE**

PREP + COOK TIME 20 MINUTES
SERVES 4

Heat 1 tablespoon olive oil in a medium heavy-based saucepan; cook 6 thinly sliced green onions (scallions), stirring, until softened. Add 2½ teaspoons finely grated fresh ginger and 1½ cups basmati rice; stir to coat in oil. Add 2 cups chicken stock; bring to the boil. Reduce heat to low; simmer, covered, for 10 minutes. Remove from heat; stand, covered, for 5 minutes, then fluff with fork. Stir in 2 tablespoons finely chopped fresh mint; season to taste.

COCONUT **RICE**

PREP + COOK TIME 20 MINUTES
SERVES 4

Place 1½ cups jasmine rice, 270ml canned coconut milk, ⅔ cup water and 2 teaspoons finely grated fresh ginger in a heavy-based saucepan; stir well to combine. Season with salt. Cover pan with a lid; bring to the boil over medium heat. Reduce heat to low; cook for 10 minutes. Remove pan from heat; stand, covered, for a further 5 minutes. Serve.

FLAVOURED RICE

CAULIFLOWER 'RICE' PILAF

PREP + COOK TIME 20 MINUTES
SERVES 4

Process 1 coarsely chopped medium (1kg) cauliflower, in batches, until finely chopped. Heat 2 tablespoons olive oil in a large heavy-based frying pan over high heat. Add 1 teaspoon cumin seeds and cauliflower to frying pan; cook, stirring occasionally, for 12 minutes or until cauliflower is just tender. Stir in ¼ cup coarsely chopped fresh coriander (cilantro); season to taste.

BASMATI PILAF

PREP + COOK TIME 30 MINUTES
SERVES 4

Melt 20g (¾oz) butter in a medium saucepan; cook 1 crushed garlic clove, stirring, until fragrant. Add 1 cup brown basmati rice; cook, stirring, for 1 minute. Add 1 cup chicken stock and 1 cup water; bring to the boil. Reduce heat to low; cook, covered, for 20 minutes or until rice is just tender. Remove from heat; fluff rice with fork. Stir in ¼ cup coarsely chopped fresh flat-leaf parsley and ¼ cup toasted flaked almonds.

RICE IS ONE OF THE MOST CONSUMED FOODS IN THE WORLD, MOST COMMON IN ASIAN CUISINES, WHERE IT CAN BE EATEN AT EVERY MEAL. OUR 4 FLAVOUR VARIATIONS HELP SPICE UP ANY PLAIN RICE (WITH EVEN A VEGIE 'RICE' OPTION FOR THOSE LIMITING THEIR CARB INTAKE).

BLACK BEAN LAMB & BROCCOLINI *STIR-FRY*

PREP + COOK TIME 30 MINUTES **SERVES** 4

- **1 tablespoon peanut oil**
- **600g (1¼lb) lamb backstrap (eye of loin), sliced thinly against the grain**
- **1 clove garlic, chopped finely**
- **1 teaspoon finely grated ginger**
- **300g (9½oz) broccolini, trimmed, halved lengthways**
- **300g (9½oz) green beans, halved lengthways**
- **300g (9½oz) snow peas, trimmed**
- **⅔ cup (160ml) water**
- **½ cup (125ml) black bean sauce**
- **4 green onions (scallions), cut into 3cm (1¼in) lengths**
- **1 teaspoon sambal oelek (optional)**

1 Heat a wok over high heat, add half the oil; stir-fry lamb, in batches, until browned all over. Transfer to a medium bowl.

2 Heat remaining oil in wok; stir-fry garlic, ginger, broccolini, beans, snow peas and half the water for 3 minutes or until vegetables are tender. Transfer to another bowl.

3 Return lamb to wok with black bean sauce and the remaining water; stir-fry until lamb is heated through and coated in sauce.

4 Return vegetables to wok with green onion and sambal oelek; stir-fry to combine.

tip Sprinkle with sliced fresh long green chilli, snow pea sprouts and crunchy combo sprouts, available from major supermarkets and greengrocers, before serving, if you like.

do ahead Lamb can be marinated a day ahead; cover and refrigerate.

even faster Swap beef for lamb and use purchased beef stir-fry strips to save time, if preferred.

serving suggestion As a change from steamed white rice, serve this with steamed Chinese-style buns, available from the freezer section of Asian food stores.

BEEF WITH BLACK BEAN SAUCE, CIRCA 1978

TO GIVE THIS RECIPE AN UPDATE WE OMITTED THE ONION AND CAPSICUM CHUNKS IN FAVOUR OF THE CRISPNESS OF BROCCOLINI, GREEN BEANS AND SNOW PEAS. WE ADDED MORE SPICE WITH THE SAMBAL OELEK, WHICH GIVES A MILD CHILLI HIT, WHILE THE CRUNCHY COMBO SPROUTS ADD CRUNCH AND TEXTURE.

GADO-GADO TEMPEH STIR-FRY
LETTUCE CUPS

PREP + COOK TIME 30 MINUTES **SERVES** 4

- ½ cup (140g) smooth peanut butter (see tips)
- ½ cup (125ml) coconut milk
- ¼ cup (60ml) water
- 2 tablespoons light soy sauce
- 1 clove garlic, crushed
- 1 fresh long red chilli, seeded, chopped finely
- ½ cup (125ml) vegetable oil
- 250g (8oz) tempeh, diced
- 300g (9½oz) broccoli, stalks chopped finely, cut into small florets
- 1 medium carrot (120g), sliced thinly
- 300g (9½oz) snow peas, trimmed
- 3 green onions (scallions), sliced thinly
- 4 eggs
- 8 butter lettuce leaves (see tips)
- lemon wedges, to serve

1 Whisk peanut butter, coconut milk, the water, soy sauce, garlic and half the chilli until combined.

2 Heat 2 tablespoons of the oil in a large wok over high heat. Stir-fry tempeh for 5 minutes or until golden. Transfer to a large bowl; keep warm.

3 Heat another 2 tablespoons of oil in wok. Stir-fry broccoli, carrot, snow peas and green onion for 4 minutes or until tender. Add ¼ cup (60ml) of the sauce and toss to coat the vegetables. Transfer vegetable mixture to bowl of tempeh; stir gently to mix.

4 Heat remaining oil, 2 tablespoons of the sauce and remaining chilli in wok over medium heat. Fry eggs for 3 minutes or until the whites are firm, edges are crisp and the yolks are cooked to your liking.

5 Divide lettuce cups, tempeh mixture and chilli-fried eggs among plates; drizzle with remaining sauce. Season with pepper; serve with lemon wedges.

tips Use a sugar-free peanut butter for the sauce and serve sprinkled with coarsely chopped roasted peanuts and extra sliced green onion, if you like. Omit the chilli, if you prefer. You could also use iceberg or baby cos (romaine) lettuce leaves instead of butter lettuce, if you prefer.

SPICED LAMB & QUINOA BIRYANI
WITH CORIANDER YOGHURT

PREP + COOK TIME 35 MINUTES (+ REFRIGERATION) **SERVES** 4

- 1¼ cups (350g) Greek-style yoghurt
- 2 tablespoons finely grated fresh ginger
- 2 cloves garlic, crushed
- 2 teaspoons turmeric
- ¼ teaspoon ground cardamom
- 600g (1¼lb) lamb backstraps (eye of loin)
- 1 cup (200g) tri-coloured quinoa
- 2 cups (500ml) water
- ⅓ cup (80ml) vegetable oil

- 2 medium onions (300g), sliced thinly
- 400g (12½oz) cauliflower, cut into small florets
- 400g (12½oz) butternut pumpkin, peeled, diced finely
- 1 cup (120g) frozen peas
- ¼ cup finely chopped fresh coriander (cilantro)
- ¼ cup (45g) pistachios, toasted, chopped coarsely
- lemon wedges, to serve

1 Combine ½ cup of the yoghurt, the ginger, garlic, turmeric and cardamom in a large bowl; season. Add lamb and toss to coat. Cover; refrigerate for at least 15 minutes for flavours to develop.

2 Meanwhile, place quinoa and the water in a small heavy-based saucepan; bring to the boil. Reduce heat to medium; cook, covered, for 15 minutes or until tender. Keep warm.

3 Heat 2 tablespoons of the oil in a large wok over high heat. Drain lamb from marinade; discard marinade. Cook lamb, without stirring, for 3 minutes on each side for medium or until cooked as desired. Remove from wok; cover to keep warm.

4 Heat remaining oil in wok. Stir-fry onion, cauliflower and pumpkin for 10 minutes or until pumpkin is tender. Add peas and quinoa, season to taste; stir-fry for 1 minute to combine.

5 Slice lamb thickly on the diagonal. Combine remaining yoghurt and coriander in a small bowl; season to taste. Top quinoa mixture with lamb, dollops of coriander yoghurt and pistachios. Serve with remaining coriander yoghurt and lemon wedges.

tips You could use lamb leg steaks or beef rump steak instead of backstrap. Sprinkle with coriander (cilantro) cress or extra chopped coriander before serving, if you like.

do ahead Lamb can be marinated a day ahead; cover and refrigerate.

LAMB BIRYANI, CIRCA 1997

To give this recipe an update we replaced the classic white basmati rice with tri-coloured quinoa, threw in cauliflower, butternut pumpkin and peas, then tossed the lot in a wok, so dinner is on the table in a quarter of the time of a traditional biryani.

LIME-GINGER PORK STIR-FRY
WITH SWEET CHILLI DRESSING

PREP + COOK TIME 40 MINUTES (+ REFRIGERATION) **SERVES** 4

- 600g (1¼lb) pork fillets, sliced thinly against the grain
- 2 teaspoons finely grated lime rind
- ¼ cup (60ml) fresh lime juice
- 2 teaspoons grated fresh ginger
- 4 medium carrots (480g)
- olive-oil spray
- 1 cup (80g) shredded white cabbage
- 1 cup (80g) shredded red cabbage
- ½ cup fresh coriander (cilantro) leaves
- 4 green onions (scallions), sliced thinly

- ⅓ cup (50g) coarsely chopped roasted unsalted cashews
- ¼ cup fresh vietnamese mint leaves
- lime wedges, to serve

SWEET CHILLI DRESSING
- 1 tablespoon fish sauce
- 1 tablespoon sweet chilli sauce
- 2 tablespoons fresh lime juice
- 2 tablespoons coarsely chopped coriander
- 1 fresh small red chilli, chopped finely (optional)

1 Place pork in a medium bowl with lime rind, juice and ginger; toss to coat pork in mixture. Cover; refrigerate for 3 hours or overnight.

2 Meanwhile, make sweet chilli dressing.

3 Using a vegetable spiraliser, cut carrots into long spirals (see tips).

4 Heat a wok or large frying pan over high heat. Spray pork with oil, stir-fry, in batches, for 5 minutes or until cooked through. Transfer to a large bowl; cover to keep warm.

5 Add carrot, cabbage, coriander, green onion and dressing to bowl with pork; toss gently to combine. Top with peanuts and mint. Serve with lime wedges.

SWEET CHILLI DRESSING Place ingredients in a screw-top jar; shake well.

tip Use a spiraliser, mandoline or V-slicer to cut the carrot into long spirals or cut into julienne, if preferrred.

even faster Using a packet of prepared coleslaw mix instead of cutting the carrots and cabbage, will make this even speedier.

SALT & PEPPER TOFU WITH
SUGAR SNAP PEA STIR-FRY

PREP + COOK TIME 40 MINUTES (+ STANDING)   **SERVES** 4

- 600g (1¼lb) medium tofu
- 3 egg whites
- ⅓ cup (60g) rice flour
- 2 tablespoons white sesame seeds
- 2 tablespoons black sesame seeds (see tips)
- 1 tablespoon ground white pepper
- 2 teaspoons freshly ground black pepper
- 2 teaspoons sea salt
- vegetable oil, for shallow-frying, plus 1 tablespoon extra
- 2 cloves garlic, crushed
- 2 teaspoons finely grated fresh ginger
- 1 teaspoon cornflour (cornstarch)
- ⅓ cup (80ml) soy sauce
- 200g (6½oz) sugar snap peas, trimmed
- 170g (5½oz) asparagus, trimmed, halved
- ½ baby wombok (napa cabbage) (350g), sliced
- ⅓ cup (80ml) vegetarian oyster sauce
- 2 tablespoons mirin

1 Line a plate with paper towel. Top with tofu; place another piece of paper towel and a plate on top of tofu. Stand, tilted, for 10 minutes to drain. Cut tofu into 2cm (¾in) thick triangles; pat dry with paper towel.

2 Meanwhile, place egg whites in a shallow bowl; beat lightly. Combine rice flour, sesame seeds, pepper and salt in another shallow bowl.

3 Lightly coat tofu in egg white, then coat in rice flour mixture.

4 Heat 1.5cm (¾in) oil in a heavy-based non-stick frying pan over medium heat. Shallow-fry tofu, in batches, for 2 minutes on each side or until golden. Drain tofu on paper towel.

5 Heat extra oil in a wok over high heat; stir-fry garlic and ginger for 1 minute or until fragrant. Add combined cornflour and soy sauce to wok with remaining ingredients; stir-fry until sauce boils and thickens slightly. Remove from heat.

6 Serve stir-fry topped with salt and pepper tofu. Sprinkle with micro radish leaves, if you like.

tips Tofu is perfect encased in this crunchy peppery coating, as it creates a great textural contrast between the crispness of the exterior to the creamy silken interior. Pressing the tofu, then patting it dry helps to remove excess moisture, resulting in firmer, crisper tofu. Use all white sesame seeds if preferred. For a non-vegetarian option, swap tofu for 600g sliced and scored calamari tubes and use regular oyster sauce instead, if preferred.

serving suggestion Serve with steamed rice.

THAI-STYLE CHICKEN FILLED *OMELETTES*

PREP + COOK TIME 40 MINUTES **SERVES** 4

- 8 eggs
- ¼ teaspoon ground white pepper
- ¼ cup (60ml) fish sauce
- ¼ cup (60ml) peanut oil
- 6 green onions (scallions), chopped finely
- 600g (1¼lb) minced (ground) chicken
- 1 bunch fresh coriander (cilantro), leaves removed, stems and roots chopped finely
- 2 cloves garlic, crushed
- 100g (3oz) green beans, cut into 5mm (¼in) pieces
- 100g (3oz) snow peas, shredded
- 1 large carrot (180g), shredded
- 1 tablespoon oyster sauce
- 1 tablespoon soy sauce
- 2 teaspoons brown sugar

1 Whisk eggs in a medium bowl with half the pepper and half the fish sauce. Heat a wok over high heat. Add 2 teaspoons of the oil and 1 tablespoon of the green onion; swirl to coat.

2 Add a quarter of the egg mixture, swirling to form a 20cm (8in) round. Cook for 1 minute; transfer to a plate. Repeat with green onion and egg three times to make four omelettes in total.

3 Heat remaining oil in wok. Add chicken; cook, using a wooden spoon to break up any clumps, for 10 minutes or until browned and cooked through. Add coriander root and stems, remaining green onion, garlic and remaining pepper to wok; stir-fry for 30 seconds.

4 Add vegetables; stir-fry for 1 minute. Stir through combined remaining fish sauce, oyster and soy sauce, and sugar; cook for 2 minutes or until reduced slightly. Stir through coriander leaves.

5 Divide chicken mixture among omelettes; fold up to enclose. Serve immediately.

tips Swap pork, turkey or beef mince for chicken mince, if preferred. Instead of making omelettes, use the chicken mixture to fill iceberg lettuce cups for a Thai take on sang choy bau. Sprinkle with small coriander sprigs and extra finely chopped green onion before serving, if you like.

FRENCH OMELETTE WITH HAM AND CHEESE, CIRCA 1988

OMELETTES ARE ONE OF THE QUICKEST AND EASIEST MEALS TO PREPARE, ONCE YOU GET THE HANG OF THE TECHNIQUE. TO GIVE THIS RECIPE AN UPDATE WE TOOK INSPIRATION FROM THE FRAGRANT FLAVOURS OF THAI CUISINE INSTEAD OF THE CLASSIC FRENCH. WHILE THE OMELETTE ITSELF IS UNIVERSAL, THE FISH SAUCE, CORIANDER AND OYSTER SAUCE MAKE IT DISTINCTLY THAI – MATCHED PERFECTLY WITH THE LIGHTNESS OF FRESH CORIANDER AND SHREDDED VEG.

MISO SALMON & STIR-FRIED GREENS
WITH SOBA NOODLES

PREP + COOK TIME 35 MINUTES **SERVES** 4

- 2 tablespoons white (shiro) miso
- 2 tablespoons mirin
- 2 tablespoons light soy sauce
- 1 teaspoon finely grated fresh ginger
- ¼ teaspoon sesame oil
- ⅓ cup (95g) pickled pink ginger, plus 2 tablespoons pickling liquid
- 4 x 150g (4½oz) boneless salmon fillets
- 455g (14½oz) frozen edamame (soy bean) pods
- 200g (6½oz) green tea soba noodles
- ¼ cup (60ml) vegetable oil
- 2 bunches asparagus (340g), trimmed, cut into 4cm (1½in) lengths
- 1 bunch broccolini (175g), trimmed, cut into 4cm (1½in) lengths
- 4 green onions (scallions), cut into 4cm (1½in) lengths

1 Whisk miso, mirin, soy sauce, fresh ginger, sesame oil and ginger pickling liquid in a medium bowl until combined. Place salmon in a large bowl. Add half the miso mixture; turn to coat.

2 Blanch edamame in a saucepan of boiling water; drain and peel. Cook noodles in a saucepan of boiling water following packet directions until tender; drain.

3 Heat 2 tablespoons of the oil in a large wok over high heat. Cook salmon for 3 minutes each side for medium-rare or until cooked as desired. Remove from wok; keep warm.

4 Heat remaining oil in wok. Stir-fry remaining ingredients for 5 minutes or until tender. Add noodles, edamame and remaining miso mixture to wok; stir-fry for 1 minute or until warmed through.

5 Serve noodle mixture topped with salmon and pickled ginger.

tip Sprinkle with the Japanese seasoned spice-blend 'shichimi togarashi' and toasted white and black sesame seeds before serving, if you like.

HOISIN BEEF & SHIITAKE STIR-FRY

PREP + COOK TIME 35 MINUTES (+ REFRIGERATION) **SERVES** 4

- 1 teaspoon sesame oil
- 2 cloves garlic, crushed
- 1 teaspoon finely grated fresh ginger
- ⅓ cup (80ml) chinese cooking wine (shao hsing)
- ⅓ cup (80ml) soy sauce
- 800g (1½lb) beef rump steak, sliced thinly against the grain
- 1 tablespoon vegetable oil
- 100g (3oz) fresh shiitake mushrooms, trimmed
- 500g (1lb) choy sum, cut into 5cm (2in) lengths
- 4 green onions (scallions), cut into 5cm (2in) lengths
- ¼ cup (60ml) water
- ¼ cup (60ml) hoisin sauce
- 100g (3oz) tong ho (edible chrysanthemum) (optional, see tips)
- 1 fresh long red chilli, seeded, julienned

1 Combine sesame oil, garlic, ginger, half the rice wine and half the soy sauce in a large bowl. Add beef; toss to coat in marinade. Cover; refrigerate for 3 hours or overnight.

2 Heat a wok or large frying pan over high heat, add half the oil; stir-fry undrained beef mixture, in batches, until beef is browned and just cooked through. Transfer to a bowl.

3 Heat remaining oil in wok; stir-fry mushrooms, choy sum stalks, green onion and the water. Cover; cook for 5 minutes or until vegetables are tender.

4 Return beef to wok with hoisin, choy sum leaves, tong ho, if using, remaining rice wine and remaining soy sauce; stir-fry until leaves just wilt.

5 Serve beef stir-fry topped with chilli.

tips Tong ho is an edible form of chrysantheum available from Asian food stores; if unavailable use gai lan or spinach leaves instead. Sprinkle with snow pea sprouts before serving, if you like.

do ahead Beef can be marinated a day ahead; cover and refrigerate.

even faster To save time, use 800g purchased beef strips.

serving suggestion Serve with steamed rice or tri-colour quinoa.

FIVE-SPICE SALT & PEPPER PRAWN
STIR-FRY

PREP + COOK TIME 35 MINUTES **SERVES** 4

- 2 teaspoons sea salt flakes
- 2 teaspoons freshly ground black pepper
- 1 teaspoon chinese five-spice powder
- 1 cup (120g) cornflour (cornstarch)
- 1 cup (250ml) vegetable oil
- 1kg (2lb) uncooked prawns (shrimp), peeled, deveined, tails intact
- ¼ cup (60ml) lime juice
- 1 tablespoon fish sauce
- 1 tablespoon brown sugar
- 1 tablespoon vegetable oil, extra
- 2 cloves garlic, chopped finely
- 1 fresh long red chilli, sliced thinly
- 1 stem fresh lemon grass, white part only, chopped finely
- 3 green onions (scallions), sliced
- 1 bunch broccolini (175g), trimmed, halved lengthways
- 1 medium carrot (120g), julienned
- 100g (3oz) daikon, peeled, julienned
- 100g (3oz) snow peas

1 Combine salt flakes, pepper and five-spice in a small bowl. Place cornflour in another bowl, add half the spice mixture; stir to combine.

2 Heat vegetable oil in a wok or large heavy-based frying pan over medium-high heat. Toss prawns in cornflour mixture to coat; shake away excess. Working in batches, stir-fry prawns for 3 minutes or until crisp and cooked through. Transfer to a paper-towel-lined tray to absorb excess oil.

3 For the dressing, place lime juice, fish sauce and sugar in a screw-top jar; shake well.

4 Drain wok; wipe clean. Add extra oil and heat over medium-high heat. Add garlic, chilli, lemon grass and green onion; stir-fry for 2 minutes. Add broccolini, carrot and daikon; stir-fry for 2 minutes. Add snow peas; stir-fry for a further 1 minute. Add prawns and half the dressing; stir-fry for 1 minute or until warmed through.

5 Sprinkle prawn mixture with remaining spiced salt. Serve with remaining dressing.

tip Sprinkle with sliced fresh red chilli and micro radish leaves before serving, if you like.
serving suggestion Serve with steamed brown rice.

BEETROOT LIME

BARLEY

ROCKET

Fetta

QUINOA

BALSAMIC

CUCUMBER

CHICK PEAS

MINT Spinach

AVOCADO

Paprika

TAHINI

SUPER SALADS

CHICKEN SATAY SKEWERS
WITH CRUNCHY RAINBOW SALAD

PREP + COOK TIME 30 MINUTES **SERVES** 4

- **1kg (2lb) chicken thigh fillets, cut into 3cm (1¼in) pieces**
- **¼ cup (60ml) lime juice**
- **1 tablespoon soy sauce**
- **1 tablespoon vegetable oil**
- **100g (3oz) white cabbage, shredded finely**
- **100g (3oz) red cabbage, shredded finely**
- **1 large carrot (180g), julienned**
- **200g (6oz) baby salad mix**
- **2 green onions (scallions), chopped finely**
- **¼ cup fresh coriander (cilantro) leaves**

SATAY SAUCE

- **½ cup (75g) roasted peanuts, chopped coarsely**
- **1 tablespoon light brown sugar**
- **1 cup (250ml) coconut milk**
- **1 teaspoon fish sauce**
- **¼ cup (60ml) soy sauce**
- **2 tablespoons smooth peanut butter**

1 Make satay sauce.

2 Thread chicken onto eight 23cm (9in) metal skewers; coat with half the satay sauce. Reserve remaining sauce.

3 Cook skewers on a heated oiled grill plate (or pan or barbecue), turning occasionally, for 10 minutes or until chicken is cooked through.

4 For the dressing, place juice, soy sauce and oil in a screw-top jar; shake well to combine.

5 Place cabbage, carrot, salad mix, green onion and coriander in a large bowl. Add dressing; toss gently to combine.

6 Serve skewers with salad and reserved satay sauce.

SATAY SAUCE Stir ingredients in a medium bowl until combined.

tips If you use bamboo skewers, soak them in water for at least 1 hour before use to prevent them splintering and scorching during cooking. Sprinkle with snow pea sprouts before serving, if you like.

veg instead To make this vegetarian, omit the fish sauce from the satay sauce, and use it to coat pan-fried tempeh or tofu puffs instead of the chicken skewers.

even faster To save time, use a packet of purchased coleslaw mix instead of cutting the carrot and cabbage.

serving suggestion Serve with steamed rice.

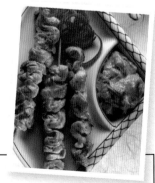

CHICKEN SATAY WITH PEANUT SAUCE, CIRCA 1988

THERE IS SOMETHING EXTRA DELICIOUS ABOUT FOOD YOU EAT WITH YOUR HANDS, AND THESE SKEWERS ARE A FAVOURITE OF CHILDREN AND ADULTS ALIKE. TO GIVE THIS RECIPE AN UPDATE WE TOOK A SHORTCUT BY MARINATING THE CHICKEN PIECES IN HALF THE SATAY SAUCE, THEN MATCHING IT WITH A CRISP, REFRESHING, EASY ASIAN-INSPIRED SALAD.

SOY-GLAZED OCEAN TROUT
SUSHI SALAD BOWL

PREP + COOK TIME 45 MINUTES **SERVES** 4

- ½ cup (125ml) soy sauce
- ⅓ cup (75g) caster (superfine) sugar
- 1½ tablespoons finely grated fresh ginger
- ⅓ cup (80ml) rice wine vinegar
- 1 tablespoon sesame oil
- 600g (1¼lb) boneless ocean trout fillets (see tips)
- 2 tablespoons teriyaki sauce
- 450g (14½oz) packaged brown microwave rice
- 1 lebanese cucumber (130g), julienned (see tips)
- 1 large carrot (180g), julienned (see tips)
- 2 small avocados (400g), halved lengthways
- 1 tablespoon sesame seeds, toasted
- ½ sheet toasted seaweed (nori), shredded finely

1 Preheat oven to 220°C/425°F. Line an oven tray with baking paper.

2 Combine soy sauce, sugar, 1 tablespoon of the ginger, 2 tablespoons of the vinegar and the oil in a small saucepan; cook marinade over high heat for 4 minutes or until thickened. Reserve half in a small bowl.

3 Place trout on tray; brush with remaining marinade. Roast trout for 8 minutes or until golden and almost cooked through.

4 Meanwhile, combine teriyaki sauce, remaining ginger and vinegar in a small bowl.

5 Reheat rice following packet directions.

6 Combine warm rice and teriyaki dressing in a bowl.

7 Flake trout into large pieces; discard skin.

8 Divide rice mixture, trout, cucumber, carrot and avocado evenly among bowls; drizzle with reserved marinade. Serve rice bowls sprinkled with sesame seeds and seaweed.

tips If you prefer, swap the ocean trout with salmon fillets. Serve with pickled ginger, if you like. Use a V-slicer or julienne peeler to cut the cucumber and carrot, if you have one.

even faster If you are short of time, replace the soy-glazed ocean trout with drained canned tuna in oil or cooked peeled king prawns (shrimp).

TEX MEX STEAK SALAD FAJITAS

PREP + COOK TIME 45 MINUTES (+ REFRIGERATION) **SERVES** 4

- **600g (1¼lb) beef rump steak**
- **⅓ cup (80ml) extra virgin olive oil**
- **2 teaspoons cajun seasoning mix**
- **½ teaspoon mexican chilli powder (optional)**
- **2 medium corn cobs (800g),**
  husks and silks removed
- **250g (8oz) mixed cherry tomatoes, halved**
  (see tips)
- **1 lebanese cucumber (130g), diced finely**
- **⅓ cup fresh coriander (cilantro) leaves**
- **1 tablespoon lime juice**
- **1 baby cos (romaine) lettuce, leaves separated**
- **12 × 25g (¾oz) mini tortillas (see tips)**

GUACAMOLE
- **1 large ripe avocado (320g), halved**
- **½ small red onion (50g), chopped finely**
- **1 large roma (egg) tomato (90g), chopped finely**
- **2 tablespoons finely chopped fresh coriander**
  (cilantro) leaves
- **1 tablespoon lime juice**

1 Brush beef with 1 tablespoon of the olive oil; rub all over with combined seasoning mix and chilli powder. Cover; refrigerate for 3 hours.

2 Cook beef, on a heated oiled grill plate (or pan or barbecue) over high heat for 2 minutes each side for medium–rare or until cooked as desired. Transfer to a plate; stand, covered, for 5 minutes.

3 Meanwhile, rub another tablespoon of oil all over corn; season. Add corn to grill; cook over medium–high heat for 8 minutes or until char marks appear. When cool enough to handle, cut kernels from cobs, in sections if possible, with a sharp knife.

4 Make guacamole.

5 Combine tomato, cucumber and coriander in a medium bowl. Whisk remaining oil and the lime juice in a small jug; season. Pour dressing over tomato mixture; toss gently to coat.

6 Thinly slice beef against the grain; season to taste. Combine beef, lettuce, tomato mixture and corn; drizzle with any beef resting juices. Serve with tortillas and guacamole.

GUACAMOLE Scoop avocado into a medium bowl; mash coarsely with a fork. Add remaining ingredients; stir to combine. Season to taste.

tips Use pork fillets instead of rump steak if you prefer and adjust the cooking time accordingly. If heirloom cherry tomatoes are not available use regular cherry tomatoes instead. Swap regular wholemeal or corn tortillas or your favourite taco shells for the mini tortillas. You can add ¼ teaspoon smoked chipotle Tabasco or hot chilli sauce to the guacamole, if you like.

do ahead Beef can be marinated a day ahead; cover and refrigerate.

'FISH & CHIP' SALAD
WITH TARTARE DRESSING

PREP + COOK TIME 55 MINUTES **SERVES** 4

- 600g (1¼lb) baby (new) potatoes, quartered
- ⅓ cup (80ml) olive oil
- ⅔ cup (55g) quinoa flakes
- ⅓ cup (45g) LSA
- 2 teaspoons onion salt
- 4 skinless boneless firm white fish fillets (600g)
- 2 gem lettuces (360g), leaves separated
- 1 small green cucumber (130g), peeled, sliced
- 500g (1lb) radishes, sliced thinly
- 2 tablespoons baby salted capers, rinsed
- ½ cup fresh flat-leaf parsley leaves

TARTARE DRESSING

- ⅓ cup (95g) Greek-style yoghurt
- ⅓ cup (100g) whole-egg mayonnaise
- 1 medium lemon (140g), juiced
- 3 small sweet spiced gherkins (45g), chopped finely
- 2 tablespoons finely chopped fresh flat-leaf parsley
- 2 tablespoons water

1 Preheat oven to 220°C/425°F. Line an oven tray with baking paper.

2 Place potatoes on tray. Drizzle with 1½ tablespoons of the oil; season. Roast, turning halfway, for 30 minutes or until golden and cooked through.

3 Meanwhile, make tartare dressing.

4 Combine quinoa flakes, LSA and onion salt in a large shallow bowl. Press fish into mixture to coat evenly. Heat remaining oil in a large non-stick frying pan over high heat; cook fish for 3 minutes each side or until golden and cooked through.

5 Place lettuce, cucumber and radish in a large bowl; toss to combine. Transfer salad to a large platter. Top with roasted potato, flaked fish, capers and parsley; season to taste. Drizzle with half the dressing; serve with remaining dressing.

TARTARE DRESSING Place ingredients in a bowl; stir to combine well. Season.

tips We used blue-eye trevalla here, but you can use any firm white fish, such as snapper, ling or whiting, for this recipe; choose thick fillets. Serve salad with char-grilled lemon halves, if you like.

MEXICAN CHICKEN SALAD

PREP + COOK TIME 40 MINUTES (+ STANDING) **SERVES** 4

- 500g (1lb) chicken breast fillets
- 1 tablespoon sweet paprika
- 1 tablespoon ground cumin
- 1 tablespoon ground coriander
- 1 teaspoon dried oregano
- 1 teaspoon garlic powder
- 1 teaspoon mexican chilli powder
- ¼ cup (60ml) extra virgin olive oil
- ½ cup (100g) white quinoa, rinsed
- 1 cup (250ml) water
- 2 medium corn cobs (800g), husks and silks removed
- 400g (12½oz) canned red kidney beans, drained, rinsed
- 1 small red onion (100g), sliced thinly
- 250g (8oz) mixed cherry tomatoes, halved
- 1 cup fresh coriander (cilantro) leaves, chopped coarsely
- 50g (1½oz) mixed salad leaves
- ¼ cup (60ml) lime juice
- 1 large avocado (320g), sliced
- lime wedges, to serve

1 Combine chicken, spices and 1 tablespoon of the oil in a large bowl; toss to coat.

2 Place quinoa and the water in a small heavy-based saucepan over medium–high heat; bring to the boil. Reduce heat to low; simmer, covered, for 10 minutes. Remove from heat; stand, covered for 10 minutes. Fluff quinoa with a fork; season to taste.

3 Meanwhile, cook chicken on a heated oiled grill plate (or barbecue or grill) over medium–high heat for 6 minutes each side or until cooked through. Stand, covered, for 5 minutes or until ready to use; slice thickly.

4 Add corn to grill; cook for 10 minutes, turning until tender and char marks appear. Cut sections of kernels from cobs, taking care to keep them intact where possible.

5 Combine quinoa, corn, kidney beans, onion, tomato, coriander and salad leaves in a large bowl.

6 Combine lime juice and remaining oil in a small jug; season to taste. Add 2 tablespoons to the quinoa mixture; toss to coat well.

7 Transfer quinoa mixture to a large platter or bowl; drizzle with remaining dressing. Top with avocado and season to taste; serve with chicken and lime wedges.

tips Replace the spices with a packet of taco seasoning mix, if you prefer. Serve salad sprinkled with coriander sprigs, if you like.

SESAME PRAWN 'TOAST' NOODLE SALAD

PREP + COOK TIME 50 MINUTES **SERVES** 4

- **800g (1½lb) uncooked prawns (shrimp), peeled, deveined, tails intact**
- **½ clove garlic**
- **1 tablespoon light soy sauce**
- **12 wonton wrappers (see tips)**
- **olive-oil spray**
- **2 tablespoons black sesame seeds**
- **¼ cup (60ml) sesame oil**
- **2 tablespoons fish sauce**
- **2 limes (130g), rind finely grated, juiced**
- **½ bunch fresh coriander (cilantro), roots and stalks finely chopped, leaves reserved**
- **¼ cup (70g) finely grated palm sugar**
- **2 tablespoons finely chopped fresh ginger**
- **200g (6½oz) dried rice stick noodles**
- **250g (8oz) snow peas, trimmed, halved lengthways**
- **230g (7oz) baby corn, halved lengthways**
- **lime wedges, to serve**

1 Preheat oven to 180°C/350°F. Line a large oven tray with baking paper.

2 Remove tails from half the prawns; reserve prawns with tails intact. Process peeled prawns, garlic and soy sauce in a small food processor until a smooth paste forms.

3 Place wonton wrappers on a clean work surface. Spread 2 teaspoons of prawn mixture on each wrapper, spreading towards edges. Spray lightly with oil; sprinkle evenly with sesame seeds. Transfer wrappers to lined tray; bake for 15 minutes or until crisp on the base and browned.

4 Meanwhile, for the dressing, combine sesame oil, fish sauce, lime juice, coriander stalks, palm sugar and ginger in a small bowl.

5 Place noodles in a large bowl, cover with boiling water; stand for 2 minutes to soften. Drain well; return to bowl.

6 Spray a large heavy-based frying pan with oil; cook reserved prawns over high heat, turning, for 3 minutes or until just cooked through. Transfer to a bowl. Add snow peas and baby corn to pan; cook, stirring, for 2 minutes or until just tender. Stir in lime rind; season with pepper.

7 Add dressing, prawns and vegetable mixture to noodles; mix well to combine.

8 Serve noodle salad topped with coriander leaves and sesame prawn 'toasts'.

tips You will need half a packet of wonton wrappers for this recipe. If you like a bit of spice add ½ teaspoon dried chilli flakes to the dressing.

even faster You could omit the prawn 'toasts' if you like and pan-fry all the prawns, or use purchased cooked king prawns instead.

PRAWNS ON TOAST, CIRCA 1978

To give this recipe an update we ditched the sliced white bread and kept the deep-fryer in deep storage. Wonton wrappers replace the bread and are spread with a delicate prawn paste, rather than battered whole prawns. The recipe changes from a starter to dinner with the addition of a noodle salad.

PAPRIKA PORK SKEWERS
WITH HERBY YOGHURT POTATO SALAD

PREP + COOK TIME 1 HOUR (+ REFRIGERATION) **SERVES** 4

- **600g (1¼lb) pork fillets**
- **4 cloves garlic, crushed**
- **1 tablespoon honey**
- **2 teaspoons hot paprika**
- **¼ cup finely chopped fresh flat-leaf parsley**
- **1 tablespoon olive oil**

HERBY YOGHURT POTATO SALAD
- **16 baby (new) potatoes (640g)**
- **⅓ cup fresh flat-leaf parsley leaves, chopped coarsely**
- **⅓ cup fresh mint leaves, chopped coarsely**
- **1 clove garlic, crushed**
- **½ teaspoon ground allspice**
- **2 tablespoons lime juice**
- **¼ cup (60ml) extra virgin olive oil**
- **½ cup (140g) Greek-style yoghurt**
- **100g (3oz) watercress sprigs**

1 Cut pork into 1cm (½in) thick slices. Combine garlic, honey, paprika, parsley and oil in a large bowl; add pork, toss to coat in mixture. Cover; refrigerate for 3 hours or overnight.

2 Meanwhile, make herby yoghurt potato salad.

3 Thread pork onto skewers; cook skewers, in batches if necessary, on a heated oiled grill plate (or grill or barbecue), turning, for 2 minutes each side or until pork is browned and cooked through.

4 Serve pork skewers with salad and remaining herby yoghurt mixture.

HERBY YOGHURT POTATO SALAD Boil, steam or microwave potatoes until tender; drain, cover to keep warm. Process herbs, garlic, allspice, juice and oil until well combined. Stir herb mixture through yoghurt; season to taste. Halve potatoes, place on a platter; drizzle over half the herby yoghurt mixture, reserving remaining to serve. Top with watercress; season.

tips Swap chicken thigh fillets for pork fillets, if prefered, and use rocket leaves instead of watercress. Serve sprinkled with micro herbs, if you like.

do ahead Pork can be marinated a day ahead; cover and refrigerate.

HERB & MUSTARD PORK
LOADED POTATO SALAD

PREP + COOK TIME 1 HOUR (+ REFRIGERATION & STANDING) **SERVES** 4

- 1 cup fresh basil leaves
- ½ cup chopped fresh dill
- 2 cloves garlic, crushed
- 3 teaspoons wholegrain mustard
- ⅓ cup (80ml) olive oil
- 4 pork cutlets (940g), trimmed
- 500g (1lb) baby (new) potatoes, halved
- 1 medium orange sweet potato (400g), cut into wedges
- 4 rindless bacon slices (320g)
- 100g (3oz) curly endive lettuce (see tips)
- 1 small red onion (100g), sliced thinly
- 250g (8oz) light sour cream
- 2 tablespoons white wine vinegar
- 2 tablespoons water

1 Preheat oven to 220°C/425°F. Line a large oven tray with baking paper.

2 Finely chop ¼ cup basil. Place in a bowl with ¼ cup dill, 1 clove garlic, 2 teaspoons of the mustard and half the olive oil; season. Add pork; toss to coat. Cover; refrigerate.

3 Meanwhile, place potatoes and sweet potato on lined tray; drizzle with remaining oil, season. Roast, turning once, for 45 minutes or until golden and tender.

4 Heat a large oiled frying pan over medium heat. Drain pork; discard marinade. Cook pork for 4 minutes on each side or until just cooked through. Rest, covered loosely with foil.

5 Meanwhile, cook bacon in same pan over high heat for 3 minutes on each side or until browned; tear or crumble into pieces.

6 Place lettuce, onion, remaining basil and dill and roasted potatoes in a large bowl; toss to combine.

7 For the dressing, combine sour cream, vinegar, the water and remaining garlic and mustard in a small bowl; season to taste.

8 Divide potato salad among plates; top with pork and bacon. Drizzle with dressing; reserve remaining to serve.

tips Use butter (boston) lettuce or your favourite mixed salad leaves instead of curly endive, if preferred. Toss the salad with half of the dressing and drizzle the pork with the remainder, if you like.

do ahead Pork can be marinated a day ahead; cover and refrigerate.

ZUCCHINI 'SPAGHETTI' & BAKED FETTA
SALAD WITH CHICKPEA CROÛTONS

PREP + COOK TIME 55 MINUTES **SERVES** 4

- **500g (1lb) cherry truss tomatoes**
- **⅓ cup (80ml) extra virgin olive oil**
- **¼ cup fresh oregano leaves**
- **200g (6½oz) piece fetta,**
  sliced into 4 lengthways
- **¼ teaspoon dried chilli flakes (optional)**
- **5 small zucchini (450g)**
- **3 cloves garlic, sliced thinly**
- **2 teaspoons finely grated lemon rind**
- **¼ cup (60ml) lemon juice**
- **2 tablespoons finely chopped**
  fresh oregano, extra
- **2 tablespoons finely grated parmesan**

CHICKPEA CROÛTONS

- **400g (12½oz) canned chickpeas**
  (garbanzo beans), drained, rinsed
- **1 tablespoon extra virgin olive oil**
- **1 teaspoon smoked paprika**
- **¼ cup (40g) smoked almonds,**
  chopped coarsely

1 Preheat oven to 200°C/400°F. Line two oven trays with baking paper.

2 Place tomatoes on one tray; drizzle with 1 tablespoon of the olive oil and sprinkle with 2 tablespoons of the oregano leaves, season. Roast for 20 minutes or until blistered.

3 Meanwhile, place fetta on second tray; drizzle with 1 tablespoon of the oil and sprinkle with chilli and 2 teaspoons of the oregano. Bake for 12 minutes or until fetta is golden.

4 Make chickpea croûtons.

5 Using a julienne peeler or spiraliser (see tips), cut zucchini into long noodles; place in a large bowl.

6 Heat 1 tablespoon of the oil in a small frying pan over medium heat; cook garlic for 2 minutes or until lightly golden. Stir in rind, juice, remaining oil, extra chopped oregano and the parmesan.

7 Add garlic mixture, roasted tomatoes with any cooking juices and remaining oregano leaves to zucchini; toss to combine. Season to taste. Serve zucchini mixture topped with fetta and chickpea croûtons.

CHICKPEA CROÛTONS Combine ingredients in a medium bowl. Cook chickpea mixture in a large heavy-based frying pan over high heat, stirring, for 14 minutes or until crisp. Cool.

tips To create the long pasta-like strands, you will need a julienne peeler, which looks like a wide-bladed vegetable peeler with a serrated rather than straight blade. Alternatively, use a spiraliser, a hand-cranked machine designed to cut vegetables into noodles or ribbons. Both items are available from kitchenware shops. You can omit the chickpea croûtons and serve this with chargrilled sourdough slices, if you like.

CHARGRILLED STEAK, MUSHROOM & BEETROOT SALAD

PREP + COOK TIME 40 MINUTES **SERVES** 4

- **500g (1lb) baby beetroot (beets), with leaves attached, reserved**
- **1 bunch baby (dutch) carrots (400g), trimmed, peeled, leaves reserved**
- **2 medium red onions (340g), cut into wedges**
- **4 portobello mushrooms (200g)**
- **1 bunch asparagus (170g), trimmed**
- **2 tablespoons olive oil**
- **4 x 250g (8oz) beef eye fillet steaks**

MUSTARD VINAIGRETTE

- **2 teaspoons dijon mustard**
- **1 clove garlic, crushed**
- **2 teaspoons caster (superfine) sugar**
- **¼ cup (60ml) red wine vinegar**
- **½ cup (125ml) extra virgin olive oil**

1 Preheat oven to 220°C/425°F. Line two oven trays with baking paper.

2 Place vegetables in a large bowl, add 1 tablespoon of the oil; season and toss to coat. Divide beetroot, carrots, onion and mushrooms between trays; roast, turning occasionally, for 30 minutes or until tender and browned. Add asparagus to a tray for last 5 minutes of cooking time.

3 Meanwhile, heat a grill plate (or pan or barbecue) over medium–high heat. Brush steaks with remaining oil and season well; grill for 4 minutes on each side for medium rare or until cooked as desired. Transfer to a plate, cover loosely with foil; rest.

4 Meanwhile, make mustard vinaigrette.

5 Slice steaks thinly on the diagonal. Divide roasted vegetables, beetroot and carrot leaves among four plates; top evenly with steak. Drizzle with vinaigrette, season to taste.

MUSTARD VINAIGRETTE Whisk together mustard, garlic, sugar and vinegar in a small bowl; season. Gradually whisk in oil until well emulsified (or process in a small food processor). (Makes ¾ cup)

tips Any leftover vinaigrette can be stored in a screw-top jar in the fridge for up to 1 week. Swap a bunch of broccolini for the asparagus, if preferred. Use your favourite steak cut and adjust the cooking time accordingly.

LAMB & HALOUMI SKEWERS
WITH ROAST VEGETABLE & BARLEY SALAD

PREP + COOK TIME 1 HOUR 10 MINUTES (+ STANDING) **SERVES** 4

- 400g (12½oz) lamb backstraps (eye of loin), cut into 2cm (¾in) pieces
- 45g (1½oz) packet pistachio dukkah (see tips)
- 2 tablespoons olive oil
- 2 tablespoons lemon juice
- 250g (8oz) haloumi, cut into 2cm (¾in) pieces
- fresh mint leaves, coriander (cilantro) sprigs and lemon cheeks, to serve

ROAST VEGETABLE & BARLEY SALAD

- 1 large head broccoli (400g), cut into small florets
- 400g (12½oz) kent pumpkin, cut into thin wedges
- 400g (12½oz) canned chickpeas (garbanzo beans), drained, rinsed
- 3 cloves garlic, crushed
- 1 tablespoon ground cumin
- ¼ cup (60ml) extra virgin olive oil
- 1 cup (200g) pearl barley (see tips)
- 3 cups (750ml) water
- ¾ teaspoon pomegranate molasses
- 1 tablespoon lemon juice
- 60g (2oz) mixed salad leaves

1 Make roast vegetable and barley salad.

2 Meanwhile, combine lamb, dukkah, oil and lemon juice in a large bowl; season. Marinate for 15 minutes.

3 Pat haloumi dry with paper towel. Thread lamb and haloumi alternately onto eight skewers. Cook skewers on a heated oiled grill plate (or pan or barbecue) over high heat, turning, for 8 minutes or until browned all over and lamb is medium or until cooked as desired.

4 Transfer salad to a large platter and top with lamb and haloumi skewers; season. Sprinkle with mint and coriander; serve with lemon cheeks.

ROAST VEGETABLE & BARLEY SALAD Preheat oven to 180°C/350°F. Place broccoli, pumpkin, chickpeas, 2 cloves of garlic, cumin and 2 tablespoons of the oil in a large bowl; toss to coat. Transfer vegetable mixture to a baking-paper-lined oven tray; roast for 35 minutes or until browned and tender. Meanwhile, place barley, the water and a pinch of salt in a medium saucepan; bring to the boil. Reduce heat to low; cook, covered, for 30 minutes or until barley is tender and the water is absorbed. Cool. For the dressing, combine pomegranate molasses, lemon juice, remaining oil and garlic in a small jug; season to taste. Just before serving, combine barley, dressing and salad leaves in a bowl; top with roasted vegetables and chickpeas. Season to taste.

tips Pistachio dukkah spice mix is available in the spice section of major supermarkets; if unavailable, use your favourite dukkah, za'atar or 1 tablespoon each ground cumin and coriander. For the skewers to cook evenly, the lamb and haloumi need to be cut into same-sized pieces. Cut the lamb into 24 x 2cm (¾in) pieces and the haloumi into sixteen 2cm (¾in) pieces. You will need eight skewers for this; soak in cold water for at least 1 hour before using to prevent them splintering and scorching during cooking. You can use quinoa instead of barley, if you like.

BALSAMIC & GARLIC DRESSING

PREP TIME 5 MINUTES
MAKES 1¼ CUPS

Whisk 2 tablespoons balsamic vinegar,
¼ cup lemon juice, 1 crushed clove
garlic and ¾ cup olive oil in a small
bowl until combined.

FRENCH DRESSING

PREP TIME 5 MINUTES
MAKES 1⅓ CUPS

Combine ⅓ cup white wine vinegar,
2 teaspoons dijon mustard and
½ teaspoon caster (superfine) sugar
in a small bowl. Gradually add ⅔ cup
olive oil in a thin, steady stream,
whisking continuously until thickened.

SALAD DRESSINGS

CREAMY RANCH
DRESSING

PREP TIME 5 MINUTES
MAKES 1½ CUPS

Blend ½ cup mayonnaise, ¼ cup buttermilk, 1 tablespoon white wine vinegar, 1 finely chopped shallot, 1 crushed clove garlic, 1 tablespoon each finely chopped fresh chives and fresh flat-leaf parsley and ¼ teaspoon sweet paprika until combined.

TAHINI HERB **DRESSING**

PREP TIME 5 MINUTES
MAKES 1 CUP

Combine ½ cup tahini, ¼ cup lemon juice, 1 clove crushed garlic, ¼ cup cold water, 2 tablespoons finely chopped fresh coriander (cilantro) and 2 tablespoons finely chopped fresh mint in a small bowl until emulsified; season to taste.

COMMERCIAL DRESSINGS BOUGHT FROM SUPERMARKETS CAN BE FULL OF ADDED SUGARS AND HIDDEN PRESERVATIVES. OUR DRESSINGS ARE NOT ONLY DELICIOUS BUT EASY TO WHIP UP (AND PRETTY AFFORDABLE TO BOOT), TO TAKE YOUR SIMPLE GARDEN SALAD TO THE NEXT LEVEL

BARBECUED LAMB,
BLACK RICE & KALE SALAD

PREP + COOK TIME 1 HOUR 5 MINUTES (+ REFRIGERATION & STANDING) **SERVES** 4

- 2 cups (500ml) buttermilk
- ¼ cup (60ml) red wine vinegar
- 1 tablespoon honey
- 5 cloves garlic, crushed
- 1.5kg (3lb) piece butterflied leg of lamb
- 1 cup (210g) black rice (see tips)
- olive-oil spray
- 3 medium corn cobs (1.2kg), husks and silks removed
- 2 large lemons (400g), halved
- 1 bunch asparagus (170g), trimmed, halved
- 1 bunch kale (250g), stalks removed
- 5 radishes (175g), cut into wedges
- 3 drained cornichons (45g), sliced thinly
- 1 cup fresh dill, chopped

1 Combine half the buttermilk, 1½ tablespoons of the vinegar, honey and 4 garlic cloves in a large glass bowl. Add lamb, turn to coat well in marinade. Cover; refrigerate for 3 hours or overnight. Remove lamb from fridge 1 hour before cooking to bring to room temperature; discard excess marinade.

2 Preheat a barbecue grill plate (or pan or barbecue) on medium heat for 10 minutes (see tips).

3 Season lamb; cook on grill, turning every 5 minutes, for 35 minutes for medium-rare or until cooked as desired. Transfer lamb to a large plate, cover loosely with foil; rest.

4 Meanwhile, cook rice in a saucepan of salted boiling water for 30 minutes or until just tender; drain.

5 Lightly spray corn, lemon, asparagus and kale with olive oil; season. Grill corn cobs for 10 minutes, lemon for 4 minutes and asparagus for 1 minute; transfer each to a tray as they are cooked. Grill kale leaves for 2 minutes. Slice kernels from corn cob; place in a large bowl with rice, kale, asparagus and radish. Toss gently to combine.

6 Combine remaining buttermilk, vinegar and garlic, the cornichons and dill in a small bowl; season to taste.

7 Slice lamb thickly on the diagonal. Serve with rice salad, buttermilk dressing and grilled lemon halves.

tips If using a grill plate on the stove-top to cook the lamb, cover the pan with a piece of baking paper to prevent sticking during cooking, then cover the lamb with a large metal bowl or roasting pan for the last 5 minutes of cooking to ensure it cooks sufficiently. Instead of using black rice, you can use brown rice, quinoa, couscous or any favourite grain.
do ahead Lamb can be marinated a day ahead; cover and refrigerate.

JERK FISH & SLAW SALAD CUPS

PREP + COOK TIME 40 MINUTES **SERVES** 4

- 800g (1½lb) skinless boneless firm white fish fillets (see tips)
- 1½ tablespoons garlic powder
- 1½ teaspoons cayenne pepper
- 1 teaspoon ground cinnamon
- 1 teaspoon ground allspice
- ½ teaspoon dried thyme leaves
- 2 tablespoons olive oil
- 8 mini soft corn tortillas
- 1 small radicchio (150g), leaves separated, trimmed
- fresh coriander (cilantro) sprigs and lime wedges, to serve

SLAW
- 350g (11oz) white cabbage, shredded
- 350g (11oz) red cabbage, shredded
- 2 cups fresh coriander (cilantro) leaves
- ¼ cup (60ml) freshly squeezed orange juice
- 1 clove garlic, crushed

AVOCADO CREAM
- 2 small avocados (400g), halved
- ⅓ cup (80g) sour cream
- 2 tablespoons lime juice

1 Preheat oven to 180°C (350°F).

2 Cut fish fillets diagonally into 1.5cm (¾in) wide, 12cm (4¾in) long strips. Combine garlic powder, cayenne, cinnamon, allspice, thyme and oil in a medium bowl; season. Add fish; toss to coat well in mixture. Cover; refrigerate until required.

3 Make slaw, then avocado cream.

4 Wrap tortillas in foil, place on oven tray; heat in oven for 10 minutes.

5 Meanwhile, heat a large non-stick frying pan over high heat; cook fish, in two batches, for 4 minutes or until just cooked and golden.

6 Fill radicchio leaves with slaw and fish; sprinkle with coriander sprigs. Serve with avocado cream, warmed tortillas and lime wedges.

SLAW Place all ingredients in a large bowl; toss to combine. Season to taste.

AVOCADO CREAM Process all ingredients in a food processor or blender until combined and smooth; season.

tips We used flathead here, but you could use snapper, whiting or blue-eye trevalla fillets instead. Serve with smoked chipotle Tabasco or your favourite hot chilli sauce, if you like. You can add 2 chopped pickled jalapeños to the slaw or serve them alongside, if you like. Jerk is both the name for a Jamaican dry or wet spice seasoning featuring allspice and chillies, and the method of cooking over barbecue coals. Traditionally the seasoning is rubbed over chicken, pork and fish; use ⅓ cup purchased jerk seasoning mix instead of the garlic powder, spices and dried thyme leaves, if preferred.

do ahead Fish can be prepared 4 hours ahead to the end of step 2. Avocado cream and slaw (without orange juice) can also be prepared 4 hours ahead; add juice to slaw just before serving.

JAPANESE CRUMBED CHICKEN, EDAMAME & BROWN RICE SALAD

PREP + COOK TIME 1 HOUR **SERVES** 4

- 1½ cups (400g) brown rice
- 455g (14½oz) frozen edamame (soy bean) pods
- 2 chicken breast fillets (400g), halved horizontally
- 2 sheets toasted seaweed (nori)
- ½ cup (75g) plain (all-purpose) flour
- 2 eggs, beaten lightly
- 1½ cups (115g) panko (japanese) breadcrumbs
- ⅓ cup (50g) white sesame seeds
- ½ cup (125ml) grapeseed oil

- 2 tablespoons light soy sauce
- 2 tablespoons extra virgin olive oil
- ¼ cup (60ml) ponzu (see tips)
- ⅓ cup (100g) japanese mayonnaise (see tips)
- 5 radishes (75g), sliced thinly
- 1 medium avocado (250g), sliced
- 1 lebanese cucumber (130g), halved lengthways, seeded, sliced on the diagonal

1 Cook rice in a medium saucepan of boiling water following packet directions until just tender; drain. Place in a bowl.

2 Meanwhile, boil, steam or microwave edamame following packet directions. Cool under cold running water; peel.

3 Pat chicken dry with paper towel. Lay a seaweed sheet on each chicken piece; pat carefully so it sticks well.

4 Prepare three shallow bowls, one for flour, one for egg and one for combined breadcrumbs and ¼ cup of the sesame seeds.

5 Working in batches, coat each chicken piece lightly in flour, shaking to removing excess. Coat chicken pieces in egg, then breadcrumb mixture, ensuring they are coated evenly. Place on a baking-paper-lined oven tray until required.

6 Heat grapeseed oil in a large heavy-based frying pan over medium heat until oil registers 160°C/325°F on a deep-fry thermometer or a breadcrumb turns light golden in 1 minute. Fry one chicken piece at a time for 4 minutes on each side or until golden and cooked through. Drain on paper towel.

7 Stir soy sauce, olive oil and 2 tablespoons ponzu through rice. Add edamame, stir gently to mix; season to taste.

8 Combine mayonnaise and remaining ponzu in a small bowl.

9 Cut chicken into thick slices on the diagonal, arrange over rice salad; top with radish, avocado and cucumber. Sprinkle with remaining sesame seeds.

tips Ponzu sauce is available in the Asian food section of major supermarkets and from Asian food stores. Use your favourite whole-egg mayonnaise instead of Japanese-style mayonnaise, if you like.

even faster To save time, use two 250g (8oz) packets) microwave brown rice, if you prefer.

WIENER SCHNITZEL, CIRCA 1988

TO GIVE THIS RECIPE AN UPDATE WE TURNED TO POPULAR JAPANESE FLAVOURS BY ADDING A NORI SEAWEED LAYER BEFORE THE PANKO CRUMB COATING, THEN SWAPPING ROAST POTATOES AND STEAMED GREENS FOR A LIGHT, YET SATISFYING BROWN RICE SALAD STUDDED WITH EDAMAME.

CHICKEN & AVOCADO CLUB SALAD

PREP + COOK TIME 30 MINUTES **SERVES** 4

- **4 chicken breast fillets (800 g), halved horizontally**
- **2 tablespoons finely chopped fresh rosemary leaves**
- **2 cloves garlic, crushed**
- **¼ cup (60ml) olive oil**
- **4 eggs**
- **8 slices ciabatta bread**
- **¾ cup (90g) grated smoked cheddar**
- **8 slices pancetta (120g)**
- **2 baby cos (romaine) lettuces (400g), leaves separated**
- **260g (8½oz) grape or cherry tomatoes, halved lengthways**
- **2 medium avocados (500g), sliced**

BUTTERMILK DRESSING

- **½ cup (125ml) buttermilk**
- **½ cup (150g) whole-egg mayonnaise**
- **2 tablespoons chopped fresh chives**
- **1 teaspoon finely chopped fresh rosemary leaves**
- **1 clove garlic, chopped finely**
- **1 teaspoon finely grated lemon rind**
- **1 tablespoon lemon juice**

1 Combine chicken, rosemary, garlic and 2 tablespoons of the oil in a large bowl; season.

2 Cook eggs in a saucepan of boiling water for 7 minutes. Cool to room temperature, peel.

3 Meanwhile, make buttermilk dressing.

4 Brush bread with remaining oil. Cook on a heated oiled grill plate (or pan or barbecue) over high heat for 1 minute each side or until golden. Place on an oven tray, sprinkle with cheese; grill under a hot grill (broiler) for 2 minutes or until cheese melts.

5 Cook chicken on grill plate for 4 minutes on each side or until golden and cooked through; transfer to a plate. Grill pancetta for 30 seconds or until crisp. Cut chicken into thick pieces and break pancetta into bite-sized pieces.

6 Divide lettuce, tomato, avocado, halved eggs, chicken and pancetta among plates; drizzle with dressing, reserving some to serve. Season to taste. Serve salad with grilled cheddar toast and remaining buttermilk dressing.

BUTTERMILK DRESSING Whisk ingredients in a medium bowl until combined; season to taste. (Makes 1 cup)

do ahead Chicken can be marinated a day ahead, covered in the fridge.

BARBECUED CHERMOULLA CHICKEN
WITH FATTOUSH

PREP + COOK TIME 25 MINUTES **SERVES** 4

- 2 cloves garlic
- 1 small onion (80g), chopped coarsely
- 1 fresh small red chilli
- 1 sprig fresh coriander (cilantro), stem and root attached
- 2 teaspoons ground cumin
- 1 teaspoon smoked paprika
- 1½ tablespoons extra virgin olive oil
- 8 x 125g (4oz) chicken thigh fillets

FATTOUSH
- 180g (5½oz) marinated fetta in oil
- 2 tablespoons pomegranate molasses
- 2 tablespoons lemon juice
- 1 baby cos (romaine) lettuce (180g), leaves separated and torn
- 6 radishes (300g), sliced thinly
- 1 lebanese cucumber (130g), sliced thinly lengthways (see tips)
- 3 green onions (scallions), sliced
- 250g (8oz) cherry tomatoes, halved (see tips)
- ½ cup fresh mint leaves
- 1½ cups (45g) pitta crisps, crushed (see tips)
- ½ teaspoon ground sumac (optional)

1 Blend or process garlic, onion, chilli, coriander, spices and 3 teaspoons of the oil until almost smooth. Transfer mixture to a large bowl; add chicken, rub mixture all over chicken. Season with sea salt and freshly ground black pepper.

2 Cook chicken on a heated oiled grill plate (or pan or barbecue) for 10 minutes or until chicken is browned on both sides and cooked through.

3 Meanwhile, make fattoush.

4 Slice chicken thickly; drizzle with remaining oil. Serve with fattoush.

FATTOUSH Drain and reserve oil from fetta into a jug or small bowl; you will need ¼ cup. Whisk pomegranate molasses, lemon juice and reserved fetta oil in a large bowl; season to taste. Add lettuce, radish, cucumber, green onion, tomato and mint; toss gently to combine. Top fattoush with crumbled fetta and pitta crisps; sprinkle with sumac.

tips Use a vegetable peeler to cut the cucumber lengthways into thin ribbons. We used sweet cherry truss tomatoes here, but swap with regular cherry tomatoes, if you prefer. Pitta crisps are available from major supermarkets, some delicatessens, greengrocers and specialist food stores. Lining the grill plate with baking paper before chargrilling the chicken prevents the marinade from burning before the chicken is cooked through.

do ahead Chicken can be marinated a day ahead, covered in the fridge.

DUKKAH-CRUMBED LAMB CUTLETS
& ROASTED CAULIFLOWER SALAD

PREP + COOK TIME 50 MINUTES **SERVES** 4

- 1 small cauliflower (1kg), trimmed, cut into 1.5cm (¾in) florets
- 300g (9½oz) small orange sweet potatoes, sliced
- ¼ cup (60ml) olive oil
- ⅔ cup (90g) dukkah (see tips)
- 2 tablespoons pomegranate molasses or balsamic glaze
- 12 french-trimmed lamb cutlets (600g)
- olive-oil spray
- 1 tablespoon fresh flat-leaf parsley leaves
- 1 tablespoon fresh mint leaves
- ¼ cup (20g) flaked natural almonds, toasted lightly
- 100g (3oz) rocket (arugula), mixed salad leaves or watercress
- 1 medium lemon (140g), cut into wedges
- 1 quantity tahini herb dressing (see page 107)
- ¼ teaspoon smoked paprika

1 Preheat oven to 220°C/425°F. Line three large oven trays with baking paper.

2 Place cauliflower and sweet potato on two oven trays; drizzle with half the oil, season. Roast for 20 minutes or until golden and tender.

3 Meanwhile, place dukkah in a shallow bowl. Combine pomegranate molasses with remaining oil; rub onto lamb, season. Press lamb firmly onto dukkah to coat both sides; place on remaining lined oven tray. Spray lamb lightly with oil; roast for 12 minutes for medium-rare or until golden and cooked as desired.

4 Arrange cauliflower and sweet potato on a platter; top with lamb, herbs and almonds. Serve with rocket, lemon wedges and tahini herb dressing, sprinkled with paprika.

tip Dukkah is an Egyptian spice blend made with roasted nuts and aromatic spices. It is available from major supermarkets and delicatessens.

even faster Serve this with your favourite store-bought baba ganoush or hummus instead of the tahini herb dressing, if you like.

CRUMBED MARINATED LAMB CUTLETS, CIRCA 1988

To give this recipe an update we have replaced stodgy white breadcrumbs with the more texturally interesting dukkah spice-mix, which not only makes the cutlets look more vibrant, but gives them a more complex flavour. We have accompanied them with a healthy salad of roast cauliflower and orange sweet potato, drizzled with a fresh middle-eastern-inspired tahini herb dressing.

GRILLED BEEF
& BROCCOLINI SALAD

PREP + COOK TIME 35 MINUTES (+ STANDING) **SERVES** 4

- 2 cups (400g) uncracked greenwheat freekeh (see tips)
- 1 litre (4 cups) water
- 1 medium head broccoli (350g), cut into small florets
- 600g (1¼lb) beef rump steaks
- 1 bunch broccolini (175g), trimmed, cut into 4cm (1½in) lengths
- ¼ cup (20g) flaked almonds, toasted
- 1 fresh long red chilli, sliced thinly

HERB DRESSING
- 2 cups (120g) fresh flat-leaf parsley leaves
- 1 fresh long red chilli, seeded, chopped finely
- 5 anchovy fillets
- 1 tablespoon dijon mustard
- 1 teaspoon finely grated lemon rind
- ⅓ cup (80ml) lemon juice
- 3 gherkins (45g), chopped coarsely
- 1 tablespoon red wine vinegar
- ½ cup (125ml) extra virgin olive oil

1 Place freekeh and the water in a medium saucepan over medium heat; bring to the boil. Reduce heat to low; cook, covered, for 20 minutes or until just tender.

2 Meanwhile, make herb dressing.

3 Preheat a large grill plate (or pan or barbecue) over medium heat until smoking. Add broccoli and broccolini; grill for 3 minutes on each side or until light char marks appear. Transfer to a large bowl.

4 Grill steaks for 4 minutes; turn and cook a further 3 minutes for medium-rare or until cooked as desired. Transfer to shallow bowl with 1 cup of herb dressing; stand for 5 minutes.

5 Slice steaks thinly across the grain; return to the dressing in bowl, toss to coat. Add steak and freekeh to vegetables; toss to mix well.

6 Transfer freekeh mixture to a platter or divide among plates; top with almonds and chilli. Season to taste; serve with remaining dressing.

HERB DRESSING Process ingredients in a small food processor until finely chopped and combined. (Makes 1½ cups)

tips Use quinoa, couscous or pearl barley instead of freekeh and prepare following packet directions. You can use whatever cut of steak you prefer. Use a bunch of gai lan instead of broccolini, if you like. Add ½ cup each fresh flat-leaf parsley leaves and mint leaves to the salad and sprinkle with micro herbs before serving, if you like.

KASHMIRI LAMB SKEWERS & PANEER SALAD

PREP + COOK TIME 45 MINUTES **SERVES** 4

- 250g (8oz) paneer
- 200g (6½oz) sugar snap peas, halved lengthways
- 1 large beetroot (200g) (beets), julienned (see tips)
- 2 medium carrots (240g), julienned
- 400g (12½oz) canned chickpeas (garbanzo beans), drained, rinsed
- 2 tablespoons lemon juice
- 2 tablespoons extra virgin olive oil
- lemon wedges, to serve

KASHMIRI LAMB SKEWERS
- 750g (1½lb) minced (ground) lamb
- 3 cloves garlic, crushed
- 3 teaspoons curry powder
- 2 teaspoons ground cumin
- ½ teaspoon ground cardamom
- ½ teaspoon ground ginger

RAITA
- 1 cup (280g) Greek-style yoghurt
- 1 lebanese cucumber (170g), seeded, diced finely
- 2 tablespoons lemon juice
- ¼ teaspoon ground cumin

1 Make kashmiri lamb skewers; place on a baking-paper-lined oven tray. Cover; refrigerate until required.

2 Make raita.

3 Meanwhile, cut paneer into 1cm (½in) thick slices. Place on a tray in a single layer; pat dry with paper towel.

4 Place sugar snap peas in a large colander in the sink; pour boiling water over to blanche. Rinse under cold water; drain.

5 Arrange sugar snap peas, beetroot, carrot and chickpeas on a serving platter.

6 For the dressing, combine lemon juice and oil in a small jug; season.

7 Heat a large oiled grill plate (or pan or barbecue) over medium heat; cook skewers, turning occasionally, for 10 minutes or until browned and cooked through. Add paneer; cook over medium-high heat for 2 minutes on each side or until browned lightly and char marks appear.

8 Add paneer and lamb skewers to platter; drizzle with dressing. Serve salad with raita and lemon wedges.

KASHMIRI LAMB SKEWERS Combine all ingredients in a large bowl; season. Shape 2 heaped tablespoons of lamb mixture into an oval, then press around a skewer. Repeat with remaining mixture to make 12 skewers in total.

RAITA Combine ingredients in a small bowl; season to taste. Cover; refrigerate until required. (Makes 1¼ cups)

tips Use a julienne peeler, available from kitchenware stores and Asian food stores, to cut the beetroot and carrots into long thin strips. You will need 12 bamboo skewers for this; soak in cold water for at least 1 hour before using to prevent them splintering and scorching during cooking.

veg instead To make this vegetarian, omit the lamb and double the paneer.

do ahead The skewers can be prepared the day before, placed on a baking-paper-lined oven tray, then covered and refrigerated until you're ready to cook. The raita can be made 4 hours ahead; refrigerate until ready to serve.

serving suggestion Serve with grilled flatbread, such as naan or roti.

OLIVE OIL BASIL
GARLIC OREGANO
FENNEL
PARMESAN
CAPSICUM
POTATO
CHORIZO
PASTA TOMATOES
MOZZARELLA
PARSLEY
ONION

BEST BAKES

RED ONION TARTE TATIN
WITH CRUNCHY NUT TOPPING

PREP + COOK TIME 1 HOUR 5 MINUTES **SERVES** 4

- **2 tablespoons olive oil**
- **6 small red onions (600g),**
  halved crossways
- **4 small fresh thyme sprigs**
- **1 tablespoon balsamic vinegar**
- **1 tablespoon honey**
- **2 cloves garlic, sliced thinly**
- **150g (4½lb) ripe tomatoes,**
  sliced thinly
- **2 sheets frozen puff pastry (330g),**
  thawed
- **80g (2½oz) soft goat's cheese**
- **2 medium fresh figs (120g), quartered**
- **1 small zucchini (90g),**
  sliced thinly lengthways
- **60g (1½oz) watercress sprigs or**
  baby rocket (arugula)

CRUNCHY NUT TOPPING
- **2 tablespoons pecans,**
  chopped coarsely
- **2 tablespoons rolled rye (see tips)**
- **2 tablespoons pepitas (pumpkin seed**
  kernels)
- **1 teaspoon poppy seeds**
- **olive-oil spray**

1 Preheat oven to 200°C/400°F. Line an oven tray with baking paper.

2 Heat olive oil in a 26cm (10½in) straight-sided, heavy-based frying pan over medium heat. Add onion, cut-side up, and thyme; cook for 5 minutes. Add vinegar and honey; cook for 2 minutes. Turn onion carefully so that the cut-side faces down, top evenly with garlic; season. Bake for 15 minutes or until onion is softened. Using a lid to keep vegetables in place, drain liquid from pan into a small saucepan; reserve. Place tomato on top of onion.

3 Place puff pastry on a clean work surface; use a rolling pin to join pastry sheets together. Remove plastic and carefully lay pastry over pan; trim excess, tucking edges in around onion and tomato.

4 Bake for 30 minutes or until pastry is puffed, browned and cooked through. Cool slightly; turn out carefully onto a large plate or chopping board.

5 Meanwhile, make crunchy nut topping.

6 Bring pan of reserved cooking liquid to a simmer; simmer for 5 minutes or until syrupy.

7 Top tart with cheese, figs and crunchy nut topping. Combine zucchini and watercress in a small bowl. Drizzle tart and salad with reduced cooking liquid; serve immediately.

CRUNCHY NUT TOPPING Combine pecans, rolled rye, pepitas and poppy seeds on a lined oven tray. Spray lightly with oil; roast for 7 minutes or until light golden and crisp. Season to taste; cool.

tips Use rolled oats instead of rolled rye in the crunchy nut topping, if you like. Draining the liquid from the pan helps stop the pastry from becoming soggy, and the reduced pan juices provide a delicious dressing for the salad. The tart is best served right after baking.

SAUSAGE AGRODOLCE
& POLENTA BAKE

PREP + COOK TIME 1 HOUR **SERVES** 4

- ⅓ cup (80ml) olive oil
- 500 g (1lb) chipolata sausages (see tips)
- 3 finger eggplants (180g), halved lengthways
- 350g (11oz) mini red capsicums (bell peppers), seeded, sliced lengthways (see tips)
- 2 cloves garlic, crushed
- 1 teaspoon fennel seeds
- 2 tablespoons tomato paste
- ¼ cup (60ml) balsamic vinegar
- 3 teaspoons caster (superfine) sugar

- ½ cup (125ml) water
- ⅓ cup (60g) sicilian green olives
- ⅓ cup (25g) finely grated parmesan
- ¼ cup fresh small flat-leaf parsley leaves

SOFT POLENTA

- 3 cups (750ml) water
- 1 cup (170g) polenta (cornmeal)
- ½ cup (125ml) pouring cream
- 50 g (1½oz) butter, chopped
- ⅓ cup (25g) finely grated parmesan

1 Heat 2 teaspoons of the oil in a large deep frying pan over medium heat. Add sausages; cook, turning, for 10 minutes or until browned all over. Transfer to a paper-towel-lined plate.

2 Add ¼ cup of the oil to pan; cook eggplant, stirring, for 8 minutes or until browned lightly. Using a slotted spoon, transfer to a bowl. Add remaining oil to pan; cook capsicum, stirring for 5 minutes or until softened. Stir in garlic and fennel seeds; cook for 2 minutes. Stir in tomato paste and return eggplant to pan; cook for a further 1 minute.

3 Add vinegar, sugar and the water; bring to the boil. Reduce heat to low; cook, covered, for 10 minutes or until mixture is thickened and reduced slightly.

4 Meanwhile, make soft polenta. Preheat oven to 200°C/400°F.

5 Spoon sausages and eggplant mixture evenly over polenta, top with olives and parmesan; bake for 10 minutes. Sprinkle with parsley before serving.

SOFT POLENTA Bring the water to the boil in a heavy-based 2.5 litre (10 cup) flameproof roasting pan over high heat. Gradually add polenta in a thin, steady stream, whisking constantly until all polenta is incorporated into water; reduce heat to low. Cook, stirring constantly with a wooden spoon, for 12 minutes or until mixture thickens and polenta is soft. Remove from heat; stir in cream, butter and parmesan until well combined. Season to taste.

tips We used merguez chipolatas, but you could use your favourite chipolatas instead. Alternatively, buy regular merguez and pinch or twist them in half, then cut so they look like chipolatas. We used mini vine sweet capsicums, sold in punnets in major supermarkets; swap with 2 medium red capsicums (bell peppers), if preferred.

Serving suggestion Serve with a green salad.

SAUSAGES WITH ONION GRAVY, CIRCA 1984

TO GIVE THIS RECIPE AN UPDATE WE KEPT THE SAUSAGES AND ONIONS, THEN TURNED TO ITALY FOR INSPIRATION, REPLACING THE MASHED POTATO WITH POLENTA AND ADDING BLASAMIC VINEGAR, PARMESAN AND GREEN OLIVES. THE RESULT IS A COMFORTING, CREAMY DINNER IN A DISH, WHICH THE WHOLE FAMILY WILL LOVE.

CHICKEN PARMIGIANA BAKE

PREP + COOK TIME 50 MINUTES **SERVES** 4

- **3 cups (750ml) tomato pasta sauce**
- **2 tablespoons tomato paste**
- **600g (1¼lb) chicken breast fillets, quartered lengthways**
- **1 bunch broccolini (175 g), each cut into thirds on the diagonal**
- **200g (6½oz) yellow patty-pan squash, sliced thinly**
- **220g (7oz) bocconcini, sliced**
- **3 cups (210 g) coarsely torn sourdough breadcrumbs**
- **3 teaspoons fennel seeds, toasted, ground coarsely**
- **2 tablespoons extra virgin olive oil**
- **½ cup (40 g) freshly grated parmesan**

1 Preheat oven to 180°C/350°F.

2 Lightly grease a 2 litre (10-cup) rectangular ovenproof dish. Combine pasta sauce and tomato paste; spoon a third of the sauce mixture over base of dish. Place half the chicken on the sauce; top with broccolini, half the squash and half the bocconcini. Repeat with remaining sauce, chicken, squash and bocconcini, finishing with bocconcini.

3 Combine bread, fennel seeds, oil and parmesan in a small bowl, season to taste; sprinkle over chicken mixture.

4 Bake for 30 minutes or until top is browned lightly and chicken is cooked through. Serve immediately; sprinkled with small fresh flat-leaf parsley leaves, if you like.

tip You can use 2 thinly sliced medium zucchini instead the patty-pan squash, if you prefer.
serving suggestion Serve with a green salad .

CHICKEN & THYME ONE-PAN PIE

PREP + COOK TIME 1 HOUR (+ COOLING) **SERVES** 4

- **800g (1½lb) chicken thigh fillets, sliced thinly**
- **2 tablespoons olive oil**
- **1 large leek (500g), sliced thinly**
- **2 cloves garlic, crushed**
- **1 tablespoon fresh thyme leaves, plus extra sprigs to serve**
- **½ cup (70g) slivered almonds**
- **¼ cup (35g) plain (all-purpose) flour**
- **3 cups (750ml) chicken stock**
- **445g (14oz) sheet sour cream shortcrust pastry or 2 sheets puff pastry**
- **1 egg, beaten lightly**

1 Preheat oven to 200°C/400°F.

2 Season chicken. Heat oil in a 25cm (10in) (top measurement), 19cm (7¾in) (base measurement) ovenproof frying pan over high heat; cook chicken, in batches, stirring occasionally, for 3 minutes or until browned. Remove chicken from pan.

3 Cook leek in same pan, stirring occasionally, for 3 minutes or until softened. Add garlic, thyme and almonds; cook, stirring, for 1 minute or until fragrant. Return chicken to pan with flour; cook, stirring, for 1 minute. Gradually stir in stock; bring to the boil. Reduce heat to low-medium; simmer, stirring occasionally, for 5 minutes or until thickened slightly. Season to taste. Cool for 10 minutes.

4 Trim pastry to fit top of pan. Cut pastry off-cuts into decorative shapes. Top pie with pastry shapes; brush with egg.

5 Bake pie for 20 minutes or until pastry is golden. Serve topped with extra thyme.

do ahead The filling can be made, covered and refrigerated, up to 2 days ahead. The baked pie can be frozen for up to 3 months if cooked in an ovenproof dish.

serving suggestion Serve with steamed broccolini or other steamed green vegetables.

CHICKEN PIE, CIRCA 1997

To give this recipe an update we replaced the traditional cream-based sauce with a fresh thyme and almond, stock-based sauce. The pie is then topped off with a perfectly puffed and golden sour cream pastry crust, ensuring the result is just as satisfying as the original

CHICKEN & CORN ENCHILADA BAKE

PREP + COOK TIME 1 HOUR **SERVES** 4

- 2 trimmed corn cobs (500g)
- 2 tablespoons olive oil
- 500g (1lb) chicken breast fillets, sliced thinly
- 1 medium red onion (170g), chopped finely
- 2 cloves garlic, crushed
- 1 fresh long green chilli, chopped (optional)
- 3 teaspoons smoked paprika
- 1½ teaspoons ground cumin
- 800g (1½lb) canned diced tomatoes
- 1 tablespoon lime juice
- 8 x 20cm (8in) flour tortillas
- 2 cups (240g) coarsely grated cheddar
- ¼ cup fresh coriander (cilantro) leaves
- lime wedges, to serve

1 Preheat oven to 220°C/425°F.

2 Brush corn with 1 tablespoon of the oil. Heat a grill plate (or pan or barbecue) to medium–high heat; cook corn, turning occasionally, for 10 minutes or until golden and tender. Cut kernels from cobs, in sections if possible; discard cobs.

3 Meanwhile, heat remaining oil in a large heavy-based frying pan over high heat. Cook chicken, onion, garlic, chilli and spices, stirring, for 7 minutes or until browned. Add half the tomatoes, bring to a simmer; cook for 10 minutes. Add lime juice and half the corn; season to taste.

4 Place tortillas on a work surface. Spoon chicken mixture evenly onto the centre of each tortilla. Divide 1 cup cheddar evenly between tortillas; fold to enclose filling. Place, join-side down, in a single layer, in an oiled 20cm x 30cm (8in x 12in) ovenproof dish. Spoon over remaining tomatoes, leaving ends of tortillas exposed; sprinkle with remaining cheddar.

5 Bake for 15 minutes or until golden. Sprinkle enchiladas with remaining corn and the coriander; serve with lime wedges.

even faster Use minced (ground) chicken or pork instead of sliced breast fillets.

veg instead To make this vegetarian, omit the chicken and add a 400g (12½oz) can each drained and rinsed kidney beans and black beans in step 3 when adding the tomatoes.

serving suggestion Serve enchiladas with a bowl of sour cream and a leafy green salad. Sprinkle with sliced fresh green jalapeño chilli before serving, if you like.

CHILLI CON CARNE CORNBREAD PIE

PREP + COOK TIME 1 HOUR **SERVES** 6

- 1 tablespoon olive oil
- 1 medium onion (150g), sliced thinly
- 1 medium red capsicum (bell pepper) (200g), seeded, sliced thinly
- 2 cloves garlic, crushed
- 2 teaspoons mexican chilli powder or sweet paprika
- 2 teaspoons ground cumin
- 1 teaspoon dried rigani (greek oregano)
- 750g (1½lb) minced (ground) beef
- 800g (1½lb) canned diced tomatoes
- 1 cups (250ml) vegetable stock
- 800g (1½lb) canned four-bean mix, drained, rinsed
- ¾ cup (110g) self-raising flour
- ¾ cup (125g) polenta (cornmeal)
- 90g (3oz) butter, chopped coarsely
- 1 egg, beaten lightly
- ⅓ cup (40g) coarsely grated cheddar
- 125g (4oz) canned corn kernels, drained
- 2 tablespoons milk, approximately

TOMATO & AVOCADO SALAD

- 1 medium avocado (240g), sliced thinly
- 400g (12½oz) mixed cherry tomatoes
- ⅓ cup fresh coriander (cilantro) leaves
- ½ small red onion (50g), halved lengthways, sliced thinly
- 2 tablespoons lime juice

1 Heat oil in a large heavy-based saucepan over medium-high heat; cook onion, capsicum and garlic, stirring, for 5 minutes or until onion softens. Add chilli, cumin and oregano; cook, stirring, for 1 minute or until fragrant. Add beef; cook, stirring, using a wooden spoon to break up any clumps, for 5 minutes or until browned. Add tomatoes, stock and bean mix; bring to the boil. Reduce heat to low-medium; simmer for 20 minutes or until sauce thickens slightly. Season to taste.

2 Meanwhile, preheat oven to 200°C/400°F. Place flour and polenta in a medium bowl; rub in butter. Stir in egg, cheddar, half the corn and enough milk to make a soft, sticky dough.

3 Spoon beef mixture into a 2 litre (8-cup) ovenproof frying pan or ovenproof dish. Drop tablespoons of cornbread dough on top of beef mixture; top with remaining corn. Bake for 20 minutes or until browned.

4 Meanwhile, make tomato and avocado salad.

5 Serve cornbread pie with salad.

TOMATO & AVOCADO SALAD Combine ingredients gently in a small bowl; season.

tips You can use canned kidney beans or cannellini beans instead of four-bean mix, if preferred. Sprinkle with small fresh flat-leaf parsley sprigs before serving, if you like.

veg instead To make this vegetarian, omit the beef and replace with another two cans of four-bean mix.

SHORT CAKES WITH CHILLI CON CARNE, CIRCA 1992

TO GIVE THIS RECIPE AN UPDATE WE ADDED MORE VEGETABLES, BOTH IN THE CHILLI CON CARNE AND THE TOPPING. THE ADDITION OF POLENTA AND CORN KERNELS TRANSFORMS THE TOP INTO AN EASY CORNBREAD, WHILE THE TOMATO AND AVOCADO SALAD IS A DECONSTRUCTED GUACAMOLE, AND HELPS TO CUT THROUGH THE RICHNESS OF THE CHILLI.

OREGANO LAMB, POTATO & FETTA PARCELS

PREP + COOK TIME 1 HOUR 5 MINUTES (+ REFRIGERATION) **SERVES** 4

- **8 lamb loin chops (800g)**
- **½ cup fresh oregano leaves (see tips)**
- **1 teaspoon finely grated lemon rind**
- **⅓ cup (80ml) lemon juice**
- **¼ cup (60ml) olive oil**
- **4 small cloves garlic, crushed**
- **250g (8oz) truss cherry tomatoes**
- **1 small red capsicum (bell pepper) (150g), chopped coarsely**
- **500g (1lb) baby (new) potatoes, quartered**
- **1 cup (200g) fetta, crumbled**
- **⅓ cup (60g) sicilian green olives**
- **lemon wedges, to serve**

1 Combine lamb, ⅓ cup oregano, lemon rind and juice, oil and garlic in a large bowl; season well. Cover; refrigerate for 2 hours.

2 Preheat oven to 220°C/425°F. Cut eight 50cm (20in) long pieces of baking paper, and four 50cm (20in) long pieces of foil. Lay foil first; top with two lengths of baking paper, overlapping to form a cross.

3 Divide tomatoes, capsicum and potato evenly in the centre of each baking paper cross. Top each with 2 lamb chops; drizzle over any remaining marinade. Hold edges of baking paper crossways together, just above lamb mixture; squeeze and twist slightly. Tie with kitchen string to seal; repeat with foil. Transfer parcels to an oven tray. Bake for 30 minutes or until lamb is just cooked but still a little pink in the centre and vegetables are tender.

4 Remove parcels from oven; cut string. Carefully open parcels; fold foil and paper back, tucking under slightly to prevent burning. Bake on top oven shelf for 10 minutes to brown slightly. Top each parcel with a quarter of the fetta and olives; season to taste. Bake for a further 5 minutes or until fetta is golden and lamb and potato are browned lightly.

5 Sprinkle remaining oregano over parcels, season. Serve with lemon wedges.

tip Use 1 tablespoon dried rigani (greek oregano) instead of fresh oregano for marinating the lamb, if preferred.

serving suggestion Serve with a cos (romaine) lettuce salad.

CHEAT'S PORK & FENNEL LASAGNE

PREP + COOK TIME 1 HOUR 30 MINUTES (+ STANDING) **SERVES** 8

- **400 g (12½oz) silver beet (swiss chard), leaves and stems separated**
- **⅔ cup fresh sage leaves**
- **⅓ cup (80 ml) olive oil**
- **1 kg (2lb) Italian-style pork and fennel sausages, skins removed**
- **1 large onion (200 g), chopped finely**

- **2 cloves garlic, crushed**
- **1 cup (250 ml) dry white wine**
- **800 g (1½lb) canned diced tomatoes**
- **750 g (1½lb) smooth soft ricotta**
- **¾ cup (180 ml) pouring cream**
- **1¾ cups (140 g) finely grated parmesan**
- **375 g (12oz) fresh lasagna sheets**

1 Preheat oven to 180°C/350°F. Lightly grease a 3.25 litre (14-cup) ovenproof dish.

2 Finely chop silver beet stems and leaves. Finely chop half of sage.

3 Heat 2 tablespoons of the oil in a large heavy-based saucepan over high heat. Add sausages, onion, garlic, silver beet stems and chopped sage; cook, breaking up sausage meat with a wooden spoon, for 20 minutes or until browned. Add silver beet leaves and wine in two batches; cook, stirring, for 1 minute. Add tomatoes, bring to the boil; cook for 5 minutes. Season to taste.

4 Whisk ricotta, cream and 1¼ cups of the parmesan in a large bowl until smooth; season to taste. Spread ½ cup of sausage mixture over base of prepared dish. Top with a quarter of the lasagne sheets. Spread with half of remaining sausage mixture. Top with another quarter of the lasagne sheets. Spread with half of the ricotta mixture. Repeat layering with another quarter of the lasagne sheets, sausage mixture, remaining lasagna sheets and ricotta mixture, finishing with ricotta mixture; sprinkle with remaining parmesan.

5 Bake for 50 minutes or until golden and pasta is tender; stand for 15 minute before serving.

6 Meanwhile, heat remaining oil in a small frying pan over high heat. Carefully add remaining sage leaves, cook for 30 seconds or until crisp; drain on paper towel. Sprinkle sage over lasagne before serving.

tips Use chicken stock instead of white wine, if you prefer. Using smooth ricotta sold in tubs in the refrigerator section of supermarkets achieves a smooth, fuss-free creamy topping. Omit the crisp sage leaves, if you like. Store leftovers in the fridge for up to 3 days or freeze in portion-size airtight containers for up to 3 months.

serving suggestion Serve with a simple green salad.

LASAGNE, CIRCA 1985

To give this recipe an update we took advantage of the flavour packed into Italian-style pork and fennel sausages, using the spiced meat from these as the base for the filling. No need to make a béchamel sauce, as we have whisked together ricotta, cream and parmesan for a cheat's version.

SALMON NIÇOISE TRAY BAKE

PREP + COOK TIME 45 MINUTES **SERVES** 4

- **500g (1lb) kipfler (fingerling) potatoes, halved lengthways**
- **1 medium bulb garlic, halved crossways**
- **¼ cup (60ml) extra virgin olive oil**
- **200g (6½oz) green beans, trimmed**
- **4 eggs**
- **200g (6½oz) truss cherry tomatoes**
- **½ cup (80g) kalamata olives**
- **4 x 150g (4½oz) boneless salmon fillets**

SALSA VERDE

- **1 cup fresh flat-leaf parsley leaves**
- **4 anchovy fillets in oil, chopped**
- **2 tablespoons baby capers, drained, chopped**
- **2 tablespoons lemon juice**
- **⅓ cup (80ml) extra virgin olive oil**

1 Preheat oven to 200°C/400°F. Line a large roasting pan with baking paper.

2 Place potatoes and garlic in lined pan, drizzle with 1 tablespoon of the oil; season. Roast for 20 minutes.

3 Meanwhile, cook beans in a saucepan of boiling water for 2 minutes, remove with a slotted spoon; refresh under cold water. Reserve until required. Add eggs to same pan, cook for 5 minutes; use a slotted spoon to transfer eggs to a plate. Leave to cool; peel.

4 Add tomatoes and olives to roasting pan. Drizzle with remaining oil; stir to mix well; roast for 10 minutes.

5 Push tomato mixture to one side of pan; add seasoned salmon to other side, skin-side down, making sure salmon sits directly on pan. Roast salmon for 2 minutes, turn; roast for a further 2 minutes.

6 Meanwhile, make salsa verde.

7 Add green beans and halved eggs to pan, season to taste; drizzle with salsa verde. Serve with remaining salsa verde.

SALSA VERDE Process ingredients in a small food processor until combined.

tip Sprinkle with micro herbs before serving, if you like.

BAKED 'CLAYPOT' CHICKEN
WITH GINGER & GREEN ONION

PREP + COOK TIME 45 MINUTES (+ REFRIGERATION) **SERVES** 4

- **500g (1lb) chicken tenderloins**
- **2 tablespoons light soy sauce**
- **2 tablespoons chinese cooking wine (shao hsing)**
- **1 teaspoon sesame oil**
- **1 tablespoon finely chopped fresh ginger**
- **2 green onions (scallions), sliced thinly**
- **2 cloves garlic, chopped finely**
- **½ cup (125ml) chicken stock**
- **1 tablespoon vegetable oil**
- **1½ cups (300g) white long-grain rice**
- **2¼ cups (560ml) water**
- **½ cup fresh coriander (cilantro) leaves**
- **2 fresh long red chillies, seeded, julienned**

GINGER-GREEN ONION SAUCE

- **6cm (2½in) piece fresh ginger, peeled, julienned**
- **4 green onions (scallions), sliced thinly**
- **⅓ cup (80ml) vegetable oil**
- **1½ teaspoons sesame oil**
- **2 teaspoons light soy sauce**

1 Place chicken in a medium bowl. Add 1 tablespoon of the soy sauce, the rice wine, sesame oil, ginger, green onion, garlic and a pinch each of sugar and salt; stir to coat chicken well. Cover; refrigerate for 30 minutes or for up to 6 hours.

2 Combine remaining soy sauce and chicken stock in a bowl or jug; set aside.

3 Preheat oven to 180°C/350°F.

4 Heat oil in a wide ovenproof saucepan with a tight-fitting lid over medium–high heat. Add chicken mixture; cook for 2 minutes on each side. Transfer to a bowl.

5 Wash rice in cold water until water runs clear; drain well. Add rice and the water to same pan; bring to the boil over high heat. Reduce heat to low; cook, covered for 5 minutes.

6 Place chicken mixture over rice; pour over chicken stock mixture and bring to the boil. Transfer to oven; cook, covered, for 15 minutes or until chicken is cooked through at the thickest part and rice is tender. Remove from oven; stand, covered, for 5 minutes.

7 Meanwhile, make ginger-green onion sauce.

8 Sprinkle chicken and rice mixture with coriander and chilli. Spoon a little of the ginger-green onion sauce over; serve with remaining sauce.

GINGER-GREEN ONION SAUCE Combine ginger and green onion in a heatproof bowl. Heat vegetable oil and sesame oil in a small saucepan over high heat until it starts smoking; carefully pour hot oil over green onion and ginger mixture, causing it to sizzle. Stir through soy sauce; set aside for flavours to develop.

tips If you are in a hurry, omit the marinating time. Finely grate the ginger in the sauce, if preferred. The ginger-green onion sauce also works well with steamed or pan-fried fish fillets. Serve with chilli oil, if you like, for those who like spice.

serving suggestion Serve with pan-fried fresh shiitake mushrooms and thinly sliced cucumber, if you like.

GINGER-SHALLOT CHICKEN, CIRCA 1978

Chicken is a great family dish, cheap and a guaranteed crowd-pleaser. To give this recipe an update we took inspiration from the classic Malaysian dish Hainan chicken rice, saving time by cooking the chicken and rice together. Using chicken tenderloins instead of a jointed whole chicken makes this even faster.

SPINACH & RICOTTA STUFFED
PASTA SHELL BAKE

PREP + COOK TIME 1 HOUR (+ COOLING) **SERVES** 4

- **500g (1lb) large pasta shells**
- **500g (1lb) spinach, stems removed**
- **600g (1¼lb) ricotta**
- **2 tablespoons finely chopped fresh flat-leaf parsley**
- **1 tablespoon finely chopped fresh mint**
- **pinch ground nutmeg**
- **2⅔ cups (700g) bottled tomato pasta sauce**
- **½ cup (125ml) vegetable stock**
- **⅓ cup (25g) finely grated parmesan**

1 Cook pasta shells in a large saucepan of boiling water for 3 minutes; drain. Cool for 10 minutes. Transfer to a tray.

2 Meanwhile, preheat oven to 180°C/350°F. Oil a shallow 2-litre (8-cup) ovenproof dish.

3 Boil, steam or microwave spinach until wilted; drain. Rinse under cold running water; drain. Squeeze excess liquid from spinach; chop finely.

4 Place spinach, ricotta, herbs and nutmeg in a large bowl; stir to combine. Spoon mixture evenly into pasta shells.

5 Combine sauce and stock in a jug; pour into oiled dish. Place filled pasta shells in dish; sprinkle with half of parmesan. Cover dish tightly with foil; place on an oven tray.

6 Bake for 50 minutes or until pasta is tender. Remove foil; bake for a further 10 minutes or until golden. Cool for 10 minutes. Serve topped with remaining parmesan.

tips This recipe can be made in four 2-cup (500ml) shallow ovenproof dishes. Bake, covered with foil, for 30 minutes or until the pasta is tender. Remove foil; bake for a further 10 minutes. Sprinkle with micro herbs or small basil leaves before serving, if you like.

do ahead You can make this 3 hours ahead, up to the end of step. Cover with foil and refrigerate until ready to bake.

serving suggestion Serve with a mixed leaf salad.

PAPRIKA POTATO WEDGES

PREP + COOK TIME
45 MINUTES **SERVES** 4

Place two baking trays in the oven; preheat oven to 240°C/475°F. Cut 1kg (2lbs) floury potatoes into wedges. Place wedges in a large bowl with 2 tablespoons extra virgin olive oil, 40g (1½oz) melted butter, 2 tablespoons rosemary leaves and 2 teaspoons smoked paprika, then season with salt; toss to coat. Place wedges, in a single layer, on hot trays. Roast, turning once, for 35 minutes or until golden and crisp. Season. Serve topped with ½ cup (40g) finely grated parmesan, if you like.

GARLICKY BEANS
WITH PINE NUTS

PREP + COOK TIME
20 MINUTES **SERVES** 4

Boil, steam or microwave 200g (6½oz) each trimmed baby green and yellow beans until just tender; drain. Rinse under cold water; drain. Transfer to a large bowl. Heat ¼ cup olive oil and 1 thinly sliced clove garlic in a small frying pan over low heat until garlic just changes colour. Add 2 tablespoons toasted pine nuts; stir until heated through. Serve beans topped with pine nut mixture.

VEGETABLE SIDES

STEAMED ASIAN GREENS
WITH CHAR SIU SAUCE

PREP + COOK TIME
25 MINUTES **SERVES** 4

Layer 350g (11oz) trimmed broccolini, 150g (5oz) trimmed snow peas, 2 halved baby buk choy and 1 thinly sliced fresh long red chilli in a large baking-paper-lined bamboo steamer. Steam, covered, over a large wok of simmering water for 5 minutes or until vegetables are just tender. Combine vegetables, 1½ tablespoons char siu sauce, 1 tablespoon light soy sauce and 2 teaspoons sesame oil in a large bowl. Heat 1 tablespoon peanut oil in a small saucepan until hot; pour over vegetable mixture, then toss to combine. Top with 1 tablespoon toasted sesame seeds and a thinly sliced seeded fresh small red chilli, if you like.

PEAS & PARMESAN CRUNCH

PREP + COOK TIME
20 MINUTES **SERVES** 4

Finely grate 80g (2½oz) parmesan. Line a sandwich press with baking paper, spread with half the parmesan; cover with paper. Close the lid; cook for 1 minute or until golden and crisp. Repeat with remaining parmesan. Boil 200g (6½oz) each sugar snap peas, snow peas and frozen peas, in batches, until just tender. Drain; toss with 1 tablespoon olive oil. Top with crumbled parmesan crunch.

IT'S VERY COMMON TO STRUGGLE TO EAT YOUR RECOMMENDED DAILY AMOUNT OF VEGIES. THERE ARE ONLY SO MANY GREEN SALADS YOU CAN HAVE IN A WEEK. WITH OUR YUMMY VEGIE SIDES WE GIVE YOU SOME GOOD OPTIONS TO SHAKE UP YOUR WEEKLY MEAL PLANS.

MEDITERRANEAN FISH 'PIE'

PREP + COOK TIME 1 HOUR 35 MINUTES **SERVES** 4

- **1 large fennel bulb (550g), cut into 1cm (½in) slices, fronds reserved**
- **1 large red onion (300g), cut into thin wedges**
- **1 medium bulb garlic, cloves separated**
- **¼ cup (60ml) olive oil**
- **1 large red capsicum (bell pepper) (350g), chopped coarsely**
- **2 celery stalks (300g), chopped coarsely**
- **4 stalks fresh flat-leaf parsley, stalks chopped finely, leaves picked and reserved**
- **3 teaspoons smoked paprika**
- **½ teaspoon saffron threads**

- **2 tablespoons tomato paste**
- **½ cup (125ml) dry white wine**
- **1 litre (4 cups) fish stock**
- **400g (12½oz) canned cherry tomatoes (see tips)**
- **800g (1½lb) skinless, boneless firm white fish fillets, cut into 3cm (1¼in) pieces (see tips)**
- **520g (1lb) day-old garlic sourdough bread, sliced thinly**
- **olive oil spray**
- **1 teaspoon finely grated lemon rind**

1 Preheat oven to 220°C/425°F. Line a large oven tray with baking paper.

2 Toss fennel, onion and garlic with half the oil; season. Spread over lined tray; roast for 25 minutes or until just tender. Squeeze garlic flesh from skins, reserve roast vegetable mixture.

3 Meanwhile, heat remaining oil in a 3 litre (12-cup), 30cm (12in) round flameproof frying pan or roasting pan over medium heat. Cook capsicum, celery and parsley stalks for 2 minutes or until softened. Add paprika and saffron; cook for 1 minute. Stir in tomato paste; cook for a further 1 minute. Increase heat to high; deglaze pan with wine.

4 Add stock, tomatoes and roast vegetable mixture, bring to the boil; boil for 25 minutes or until reduced by a third. Season to taste.

5 Gently press fish into tomato mixture to submerge. Generously spray sourdough slices with oil; arrange on top of fish mixture, slightly overlapping in circles. Bake on top oven shelf for 15 minutes or until fish is cooked through and bread is crunchy and golden.

6 Serve fish pie topped with reserved fennel fronds, reserved parsley leaves and lemon rind.

tips We used blue-eye trevalla, but you can use snapper, ling, whiting or your favourite white fish fillets, instead, if you like. Swap the canned cherry tomatoes with a 400g (12½oz) can chopped tomatoes, if preferred.

BAKED FISH 'N' CHIPS
WITH YOGHURT TARTARE

PREP + COOK TIME 40 MINUTES **SERVES** 4

- **2 large orange sweet potatoes (1kg), unpeeled, cut into thin wedges**
- **2 tablespoons vegetable oil**
- **1 tablespoon ground cumin**
- **1 tablespoon ground coriander**
- **1 teaspoon ground turmeric**
- **2 teaspoons coarse cooking salt**
- **¼ cup (40g) white sesame seeds**
- **⅔ cup (50g) panko (japanese) breadcrumbs**
- **¼ cup (35g) plain (all-purpose) flour**
- **1 egg**
- **800g (1½lb) skinless, boneless firm white fish fillets (see tips)**
- **60g (2oz) rocket (arugula)**
- **lime wedges and fresh dill sprigs, to serve**

YOGHURT TARTARE

- **½ cup (140g) Greek-style yoghurt**
- **2 teaspoons lime juice**
- **2 baby gherkins (30g), chopped finely**
- **2 green onions (scallions), chopped finely**
- **1 tablespoon finely chopped fresh dill**

1 Preheat oven to 200°C/400°F. Line an oven tray with baking paper.

2 Combine sweet potato and half the oil in a medium bowl; season.

3 Place sweet potato, in a single layer, on lined tray; bake for 15 minutes or until browned lightly, cooked through and crisp.

4 Meanwhile, combine spices, salt, seeds and breadcrumbs in a wide shallow bowl. Place flour in another shallow bowl. Lightly beat egg in another shallow bowl. Coat fish in flour, shake off any excess. Dip fish in egg, then in breadcrumb mixture, turning until fish is completely covered.

5 Heat remaining oil in a large ovenproof frying pan over medium heat; cook fish for 30 seconds each side or until browned all over. Transfer frying pan to oven; bake fish for 3 minutes or until just cooked through and browned.

6 Meanwhile, make yoghurt tartare sauce.

7 Serve fish with chips, rocket and yoghurt tartare, sprinkle with extra dill.

YOGHURT TARTARE Combine ingredients in a small bowl; season to taste.

tips We used flathead fillets here, but you could use snapper, ling, whiting or blue-eye trevalla, if you like. If you don't have an ovenproof frying pan, transfer the fish to an oven tray lined with baking paper before baking. Serve with extra baby gherkins or cornichons, if you like.

PARMESAN CRUMBED FISH, CIRCA 1984

TO GIVE THIS RECIPE A HEALTHY UPDATE WE SWAPPED PACKAGED DRIED BREADCRUMBS WITH A FLAVOURFUL SPICED SESAME SEED AND PANKO BREADCRUMB COATING, THEN MADE OUR OWN SWEET POTATO CHIPS, WHICH ARE BAKED NOT FRIED. WE REPLACED MAYONNAISE IN THE TARTARE WITH THE HEALTHIER OPTION OF GREEK-STYLE YOGHURT.

PORK, CRACKLING & PEAR TRAY BAKE
WITH CAVOLO NERO COLCANNON

PREP + COOK TIME 45 MINUTES (+ STANDING) **SERVES** 4

- **4 x 300g (9½oz) pork loin chops**
- **1 tablespoon olive oil**
- **1 medium bulb garlic, broken into clusters**
- **4 small pears (720g), halved lengthways**
- **8 fresh sage sprigs**

CAVOLO NERO COLCANNON

- **1kg (2lb) potatoes, peeled, chopped coarsely**
- **1 cup (250ml) milk**
- **1 bay leaf**
- **3 green onions (scallions), sliced thinly**
- **1 bunch cavolo nero (tuscan cababage) (100g), leaves stripped, chopped coarsely**
- **50g (1½oz) butter, chopped**

1 Make cavolo nero colcannon.

2 Meanwhile, preheat oven to 200°C/400°F. Oil and line a large roasting pan with baking paper.

3 Remove rind from pork, score; cut rind in half lengthways. Season rind and chops generously. Place rind and garlic in lined pan; roast for 15 minutes or until rind is crisp and garlic is golden. Transfer to a paper towel–lined plate.

4 Add pork to pan; roast for 2 minutes. Turn pork; add pears and sage. Roast for 10 minutes or until both pork and pears are tender and browned; stand, covered loosely with foil, for 10 minutes. Discard excess fat from pan, keeping any pan juices.

5 Serve colcannon topped with pork and pear with pan juices, crackling and roasted garlic; sprinkle with sliced green onion, if you like.

CAVOLO NERO COLCANNON Cook potato in a saucepan of boiling water for 15 minutes or until tender. Drain, return to pan; stir with a wooden spoon over low heat to dry potato and mash slightly. Meanwhile, place milk and bay leaf in a medium saucepan over medium heat; bring just to the boil. Remove from heat, leave to infuse for 10 minutes; discard bay leaf. Add green onion and cavolo nero to milk. Pour milk mixture over potato; stir gently to combine. Season to taste; stir in butter until well combined.

tips Use 2 quartered granny smith apples instead of the pears, if you like. We used cavolo nero (tuscan cabbage), a type of kale, and dutch cream potatoes in the colcannon, but regular kale and potatoes would work too.

CUBAN BEEF EMPANADAS
WITH CINNAMON ROAST PUMPKIN

PREP + COOK TIME 1 HOUR 20 MINUTES (+ COOLING) **SERVES** 4

- ⅓ cup (80ml) olive oil
- 1 medium red onion (170g), chopped finely
- 3 cloves garlic, chopped finely
- 1 cured chorizo sausage (170g), diced finely
- 1 large red capsicum (bell pepper) (350g), chopped finely
- 500 g (1lb) minced (ground) beef
- 2 teaspoons ground cumin
- 2 teaspoons smoked paprika
- ¼ cup (40g) currants
- 400g (12½oz) canned diced tomatoes
- 1 tablespoon tomato paste
- ½ cup (125ml) water
- 8 sheets frozen shortcrust pastry (400g)
- 1kg (2lb) butternut pumpkin, peeled, cut into 2cm (¾in) pieces
- ½ teaspoon ground cinnamon
- 1 egg, beaten lightly
- 2 tablespoons polenta (cornmeal)
- lime wedges, to serve

1 Preheat oven to 180°C/350°F. Line a large oven tray with baking paper.

2 Heat 2 tablespoon of the oil in a large heavy-based frying pan over high heat. Add onion; cook for 3 minutes or until softened. Add garlic, chorizo and capsicum; cook, stirring, for 4 minutes or until capsicum is softened.

3 Add beef to pan; cook, stirring with a wooden spoon to break up any clumps, for 10 minutes or until browned.

4 Stir in cumin and paprika; cook for 1 minute or until aromatic. Add currants, tomatoes, tomato paste and the water. Bring to the boil; cook for 10 minutes or until most of the liquid is evaporated and the mixture is thickened. Leave to cool.

5 Cut eight 25cm (10in) squares of baking paper. Cut an 18cm (7¼in) round from each pastry sheet; place each onto a piece of baking paper.

6 Place an eighth of beef filling in centre of each pastry round. Brush a little egg around edge of pastry. Fold each pastry round in half to enclose filling. Use a fork to press around edges to seal; alternatively, pleat into a neat pattern.

7 Place pumpkin on lined tray; brush with remaining oil. Sprinkle evenly with cinnamon, season. Brush top of each empanada with egg; sprinkle with polenta. Bake on centre shelf of oven with pumpkin on another shelf for 30 minutes or until empanadas are golden and pumpkin is tender and browned; check underneath empanadas to ensure pastry is golden.

8 Serve empanadas with roast pumpkin and lime wedges; sprinkle with fresh coriander leaves, if you like.

tips This makes eight empanadas. If you have any leftover, store in an airtght container in the fridge for up to 2 days and warm in a preheated 180°C/350°F oven or wrap indvidually in plastic wrap, then freeze in an airtight container for up to 1 month. For a Cuban-inspired shepherd's pie, you could use lamb mince instead of beef, then place the filling in a medium ovenproof dish, top with mashed potato or sweet potato and bake at the same temperature for 30 minutes or until browned lightly. Serve with sriracha or your favourite chilli sauce, if you like.

serving suggestion Serve with a mixed leaf and avocado salad.

SEAFOOD PAELLA BAKE

PREP + COOK TIME 1 HOUR 15 MINUTES **SERVES** 4

- ⅓ cup (80ml) extra virgin olive oil
- 1 medium onion (150g), chopped finely
- 2 medium red capsicums (bell peppers) (400g), chopped coarsely (see tips)
- 2 cloves garlic, crushed
- 2 teaspoons smoked paprika
- 2 cups (400g) brown rice
- 300g (9½oz) orange sweet potatoes, diced
- 1 litre (4 cups) chicken stock
- 1 pinch saffron threads
- 300g (9½oz) boneless, skinless firm white fish fillets, cut into 5cm (2in) chunks (see tips)
- 600g (1¼lb) uncooked large prawns (shrimp), peeled, deveined, tails intact
- 3 medium tomatoes (480g), diced
- 2 tablespoons finely chopped fresh flat-leaf parsley
- 1 tablespoon lemon juice
- fresh flat-leaf parsley sprigs and lemon wedges, to serve

1 Preheat oven to 180°C/350°F.

2 Heat 1 tablespoon of oil in a large flameproof casserole dish; cook onion and capsicum for 3 minutes or until softened. Add garlic and paprika; cook for 30 seconds or until fragrant. Stir through rice to coat grains; add sweet potato, stock and saffron. Bring to a simmer; cover with a lid.

3 Bake for 40 minutes or until rice is tender and stock is absorbed.

4 Meanwhile, heat 1 tablespoon of the oil in a large heavy-based frying pan. Cook fish for 2 minutes or until sealed; transfer to a plate. Add another 1 tablespoon oil to pan; cook prawns for 2 minutes or until sealed. Transfer to plate with fish.

5 Place fish and prawns evenly on top of rice, return to oven; cook, uncovered, for a further 5 minutes or until fish and prawns are cooked through.

6 Combine tomato, chopped parsley, lemon juice and remaining oil; season to taste. Sprinkle paella with parsley sprigs; serve with tomato salad and lemon wedges.

tips Use one red and one yellow capsicum, if you like. If your family aren't huge seafood fans but like paella, swap 600g chicken tenderloins or thigh fillets cut into 2cm (¾in) pieces for the fish and prawns, then cook for 5 minutes or until browned lightly and almost cooked through in step 2.

SEAFOOD PAELLA, CIRCA 1991

To give this recipe an update we used brown rice instead of the traditional short-grain paella rice. Instead of cooking on the stovetop in a paella pan, we used a casserole dish and baked it in the oven, taking out the margin for error in cooking the rice perfectly. Then all it needs is for the seafood to be pan-fried then added to the dish for a few final moments in the oven.

TURMERIC LAMB

THYME PUMPKIN

MINT

SALMON

PARSLEY

PARSNIPS SOY SAUCE

MISO DUKKAH

CHICKEN

LEMON

PORK

Modern Roasts

ROASTED CHICKEN 'N' CHIPS

PREP + COOK TIME 1 HOUR 15 MINUTES (+ REFRIGERATION) **SERVES** 4

- **1.6kg (3¼lb) whole chicken**
- **⅓ cup (80ml) extra virgin olive oil**
- **2 cloves garlic, crushed**
- **2 teaspoons ground cumin**
- **2 teaspoons ground coriander**
- **1 teaspoon smoked paprika**
- **1 teaspoon cinnamon sugar**
- **1 teaspoon ground turmeric**

- **½ teaspoon mexican chilli powder**
- **100g (3oz) mixed salad leaves**
- **1 tablespoon lemon juice**
- **200g (6½oz) Greek-style yoghurt**

SWEET POTATO CHIPS
- **500g (1lb) white sweet potatoes**
- **500g (1lb) orange sweet potatoes**
- **⅓ cup (80ml) vegetable oil**

1 Pat chicken dry with paper towel. Place chicken, breast-side down, on a clean chopping board. Using poultry shears or sharp scissors, cut down either side of the backbone; discard. Open chicken to lie flat. Turn, breast-side up; press firmly with the heel of your hand to flatten. Tuck wings under; place in an ovenproof dish.

2 Combine 2 tablespoons of the oil, the garlic and spices in a small bowl; mix well; season. Reserve 3 teaspoons of spice mixture; rub remaining spice mixture all over chicken. Cover; refrigerate for 1 hour.

3 Preheat oven 220°C/425°F.

4 Roast chicken for 50 minutes or until cooked through and juices run clear when a knife is inserted into a thigh joint. Cover loosely with foil; stand for 10 minutes

5 Meanwhile, make sweet potato chips.

6 Place salad leaves in a small bowl, drizzle with remaining oil and lemon juice; toss to combine.

7 Place yoghurt and reserved spice mixture in a small bowl; stir gently to combine.

8 Serve chicken with chips, salad leaves, spiced yoghurt and lemon wedges, if you like.

SWEET POTATO CHIPS Wash and scrub sweet potatoes; pat dry. Line two large oven trays with baking paper. Cut sweet potatoes into even 2cm (¾in) thick chip-sized pieces. Place on oven trays in a single layer, drizzle with oil; season. Roast sweet potato, turning halfway through cooking time, for 20 minutes or until tender, browned and crisp.

tips You can also use the spice mix to coat chicken drumsticks or thighs on the bone, then roast for 25 minutes or until cooked through. Add sliced avocado to the salad, if you like.

MODERN ROASTS

CHICKEN 'N' CHIPS, CIRCA 1988

To give this recipe an update we butterflied the chicken, then rubbed it with a spice mix that achieves a crispy skin result that is uncannily like the flavour of a takeaway barbecue chook, minus all the salt and fat. The baked-not-fried sweet potato chips also make this a healthier take on a fast food family favourite.

STICKY CHICKEN WINGS
WITH QUINOA 'FRIED RICE'

PREP + COOK TIME 50 MINUTES (+ REFRIGERATION) **SERVES** 4

- 12 small chicken wings (1kg) (see tips)
- ⅓ cup (80ml) tomato sauce (ketchup)
- 1½ tablespoons soy sauce
- 2 teaspoons honey
- 1 tablespoon sesame seeds
- ¼ cup fresh coriander (cilantro) leaves

QUINOA 'FRIED RICE'
- 1 cup (200g) quinoa, rinsed
- 100g (3oz) sugar snap peas
- 2 teaspoons vegetable oil
- 2 teaspoons sesame oil
- 150g (5oz) oyster mushrooms, torn
- 2 cloves garlic, sliced thinly
- 4cm (1½in) piece fresh ginger, julienned
- 100g (3oz) frozen shelled edamame (soy beans)
- 4 green onions (scallions), chopped finely
- 2 tablespoons kecap manis

1 Remove and discard tips from chicken wings. Cut wings in half at the joint.

2 Combine sauces, honey, half the seeds and chicken in a medium bowl. Cover; refrigerate for 2 hours or overnight.

3 Preheat oven to 200°C/400°F.

4 Place chicken on an oiled wire rack over a large roasting pan. Roast for 30 minutes or until chicken is cooked through.

5 Meanwhile, make quinoa 'fried rice'.

6 Sprinkle chicken with remaining sesame seeds. Serve chicken wings with 'fried rice', sprinkled with coriander.

QUINOA 'FRIED RICE' Cook quinoa in a large saucepan of boiling water for 12 minutes or until tender; drain. Spread quinoa on an oven tray. Refrigerate, uncovered. Boil, steam or microwave sugar snap peas until just tender. Heat combined oils in a wok over high heat; stir-fry mushrooms for 1 minute or until almost cooked through. Add garlic and ginger; stir-fry for 1 minute or until fragrant. Add edamame and snap peas; stir-fry for 2 minutes or until heated through. Add green onion; stir-fry for 1 minute. Add quinoa and kecap manis; stir-fry for 1 minute or until heated through.

tips Using quinoa gives this fried rice a low-carb makeover that is every bit as satisfying as the regular rice version. However, you can use microwave brown rice instead of quinoa, if you like.

even faster Buy already trimmed chicken wings, sold as chicken 'nibbles' in major supermarkets, and omit step 1.

do ahead Chicken can be marinated the day before and refrigerated, covered. Cook quinoa the day before and refrigerate overnight on an uncovered oven tray.

FENNEL & ORANGE SALT ROAST PORK
WITH BEETROOT & ORANGE SALAD

PREP + COOK TIME 1 HOUR 20 MINUTES **SERVES** 6

- **500g (1lb) baby beetroot (beets), leaves attached**
- **250g (8oz) golden baby beetroot (beets), leaves attached**
- **1 tablespoon coarse cooking salt (kosher salt)**
- **2 teaspoons fennel seeds, crushed**
- **2 teaspoons finely grated orange rind**
- **1kg (2lb) rack of pork (6 cutlets), rind on**
- **⅓ cup (80ml) extra virgin olive oil**
- **400g (12½oz) kent pumpkin, unpeeled, cut into thick wedges**
- **2 small oranges (180g), peeled, halved crossways, sliced thinly**
- **2 tablespoons freshly squeezed orange juice**

1 Preheat oven to 220°C/425°F.

2 Trim beetroot, leaving 3cm (1¼in) of the stem attached; discard roots and reserve small leaves. Wrap beetroot in foil; place on an oven tray.

3 Combine salt, fennel seeds and rind in a small bowl.

4 Using a very sharp knife, score rind at 5mm (¼in) intervals, cutting into the fat but not the flesh. Rub pork rind with 2 teaspoons of the oil, then the salt mixture. Place pork in a roasting pan; roast pork and beetroot for 35 minutes or until pork rind is blistered.

5 Place pumpkin on tray with beetroot; drizzle with another 2 teaspoons oil and season. Reduce oven to 180°C/350°F; roast pork and vegetables for 40 minutes or until cooked through. Remove pork from pan; cover to keep warm.

6 When beetroot are cool enough to handle, peel and halve.

7 Place beetroot, orange and reserved beetroot leaves in a medium bowl. Add combined orange juice and remaining oil to beetroot mixture; toss gently to combine. Season to taste.

8 Serve sliced pork with beetroot and orange salad and roasted pumpkin.

tips Use all red baby beetroot instead of a mix of red and yellow baby beetroot, if preferred. If the beetroot leaves are not attached, or are too large and tough, use 120g (4oz) baby beetroot (beet) leaves instead. Sprinkle with micro herbs, such as baby sorrel before serving, if you like.

even faster Swap 600g pork fillets for the rack of pork, omit the salt and rub the combined fennel seeds, orange rind and oil over the pork; roast for 15 minutes or until cooked to your liking.

ROAST CHIMICHURRI CHICKEN
WITH PAN 'UNSTUFFING'

PREP + COOK TIME 1 HOUR 30 MINUTES (+ STANDING) **SERVES** 4

- **4 medium carrots (480g)**
- **4 medium potatoes (800g), quartered**
- **1.6kg (3½lb) whole chicken**
- **2 tablespoons olive oil**
- **140g (4½oz) cured chorizo sausages, chopped coarsely**
- **1 medium white onion (150g), chopped coarsely**
- **4 cups (280g) coarsely torn wholemeal sourdough breadcrumbs**
- **¼ cup finely chopped fresh flat-leaf parsley**
- **1 tablespoon currants**
- **1 egg, beaten lightly**

CHIMICHURRI

- **2 cups firmly packed fresh flat-leaf parsley leaves**
- **1 bunch fresh coriander (cilantro), stems and leaves chopped coarsely**
- **2 green onions (scallions), chopped**
- **3 cloves garlic, crushed**
- **2 tablespoons olive oil**
- **¼ cup (30g) pickled jalapeño chillies, sliced**
- **¼ cup (60ml) jalapeño pickling liquid**

1 Make chimichurri. Reserve 2 tablespoons for stuffing.

2 Grate one carrot; set aside. Cut remaining carrots into 4 cm (1½in) lengths; place in a medium saucepan with potato. Cover with cold water and bring to the boil; remove from heat. Leave to stand for 10 minutes; drain.

3 Preheat oven to 180°C/350°F. Oil and line a large oven tray with baking paper.

4 Pat chicken dry with paper towel. Place chicken, breast-side down, on a clean chopping board. Using poultry shears or sharp scissors, cut down either side of the backbone; discard. Open chicken to lie flat. Turn, breast-side up and push down to flatten; tuck wings under. Rub chicken with 2 tablespoons chimichurri; place in a roasting pan. Place carrot and potato in another roasting pan; drizzle with 1 tablespoon of the oil, season.

5 Roast chicken and vegetables for 15 minutes; spoon pan juices over vegetables.

6 Meanwhile, heat remaining oil in a heavy-based frying pan over high heat. Add chorizo and onion; cook for 5 minutes or until softened and fragrant. Transfer to a bowl; add breadcrumbs, parsley, currants, grated carrot, egg and reserved chimichurri. Stir to combine well, transfer to lined tray; spread evenly.

7 Add stuffing to lower oven shelf. Roast for a further 45 minutes or until chicken, vegetables and stuffing are browned and cooked through; stir stuffing occasionally with a fork to ensure it cooks evenly.

8 Stand chicken, covered loosely with foil, for 10 minutes. Cut chicken into 4 pieces; serve with roast vegetables, stuffing and remaining chimichurri.

CHIMICHURRI Process ingredients until a bright-green paste forms; season to taste.

tips Roasting the stuffing and chicken separately ensures the stuffing is golden and a little crisp, while the chicken is cooked through. Sprinkle with coriander leaves before serving, if you like.

even faster For a super-quick roast chicken dinner, use three-quarters of the chimichurri to coat 1kg (2lb) chicken drumsticks, thighs or wings and use 600g baby (chat) potatoes instead of large potatoes, then adjust the roasting time accordingly. Omit the stuffing (add pumpkin wedges to the roasting pan instead) and serve with the remaining chimichurri mixed with some plain Greek-style yoghurt, if you like.

WALNUT-DUKKAH OCEAN TROUT
WITH TAHINI-YOGHURT SAUCE

PREP + COOK TIME 35 MINUTES **SERVES** 6

- **150g (4½oz) turkish bread**
- **45g (1½oz) lemon dukkah**
- **⅓ cup (35g) walnuts,**
  chopped coarsely
- **2 cups fresh flat-leaf parsley leaves,**
  chopped coarsely
- **2 tablespoons currants**
- **2 tablespoons extra virgin olive oil**
- **2 tablespoons Greek-style yoghurt**
- **1 tablespoon tahini**
- **1kg (2lb) piece skinless boneless**
  ocean trout fillet (see tips)
- **800g (1½lb) heirloom cherry**
  tomatoes, halved
- **60g (2oz) watercress sprigs**
- **lemon wedges, to serve**

TAHINI-YOGHURT SAUCE

- **2 tablespoons Greek-style yoghurt**
- **1 tablespoon tahini**
- **2 tablespoons lemon juice**
- **2 teaspoons finely chopped fresh**
  flat-leaf parsley

1 Preheat oven to 200°C/400°F. Line a large roasting pan or oven tray with baking paper.

2 Process bread to medium-sized coarse crumbs; transfer to a medium bowl. Add dukkah, walnuts, parsley, currants and oil; season to taste. Stir well so that oil coats ingredients. Combine yoghurt and tahini in a small bowl.

3 Pat fish dry with paper towel. Trim belly; discard or reserve for another use (see tips). Place on tray; season. Brush yoghurt mixture over fish. Top with breadcrumb mixture, patting down firmly to coat.

4 Roast fish for 15 minutes or until crumb crust is golden and fish is still pink in the centre or continue until cooked as desired.

5 Meanwhile, make tahini-yoghurt sauce.

6 Serve trout with tahini-yoghurt sauce, tomatoes, watercress and lemon wedges.

TAHINI-YOGHURT SAUCE Combine yoghurt and tahini in a small bowl. Add lemon juice and parsley; combine well. Season to taste.

tips Buy a whole ocean trout side fillet for this; you can use the trimmed trout belly to make a fish tartare or ceviche. Alternatively, use a salmon fillet instead. Use raisins or sultanas instead of currants, if that is what's in your pantry and regular cherry or grape tomatoes, if you prefer.

even faster Use four 200g (6½oz) ocean trout fillets or salmon fillets instead of a whole side; roast for 5 minutes or until cooked as desired.

EASY ROAST CHICKEN DINNER
WITH INSIDE-OUT STUFFING

PREP + COOK TIME 50 MINUTES **SERVES** 4

- **3 slices soy and linseed bread (120g)**
- **20g (¾oz) prosciutto slices, chopped finely**
- **⅓ cup (55g) finely chopped dried apricots**
- **2 green onions (scallions), chopped finely**
- **2 teaspoons fresh thyme leaves**
- **1 egg, beaten lightly**
- **4 x 200g (6½oz) chicken breast fillets**
- **1 tablespoon dijon mustard**
- **250g (8oz) swiss brown mushrooms**
- **2 medium red onions (170g), cut into wedges**
- **300g (9½oz) small brussels sprouts**
- **400g (12½oz) baby (dutch) carrots, trimmed**
- **2 trimmed, cleaned corn cobs (500g), halved**
- **1½ tablespoons olive oil**
- **3 teaspoons balsamic vinegar**

1 Preheat oven to 180°C/350°F. Line an oven tray with baking paper.

2 Blend or process bread into coarse crumbs. Transfer to a bowl with prosciutto, apricot, green onion and thyme. Combine with egg to loosely bind together.

3 Place chicken in a single layer on tray. Brush top and sides with mustard. Press crumb mixture all over top and sides of chicken. Roast for 10 minutes.

4 Meanwhile, toss mushrooms, onion, brussels sprouts, carrots, corn and oil in a bowl; season with pepper. Roast vegetables with chicken for a further 15 minutes or until vegetables are tender, and chicken is just cooked through and crust is golden brown.

5 Divide chicken and vegetables among plates; drizzle roast vegetables with balsamic vinegar to serve.

tips Replace the prosciutto with the same amount of ham, if you like, and use dried pear, apple or dates instead of apricots. Swap the brussels sprouts with 200g (6½oz) trimmed halved broccolini, if you prefer.

OVEN-BARBECUED PORK RIBS
WITH APPLE SLAW

PREP + COOK TIME 1 HOUR 30 MINUTES **SERVES** 4

- **1 cup (250ml) barbecue sauce**
- **¼ cup (60ml) worcestershire sauce**
- **1 tablespoon apple cider vinegar**
- **2 teaspoons smoked paprika**
- **1 teaspoon garlic salt**
- **½ teaspoon dried chilli flakes**
- **2½kg (3lb) American-style pork spare ribs, cut into 4-rib sections**
- **4 corn cobs (1kg)**
- **40g (1½oz) butter, softened**

APPLE SLAW

- **500g (1lb) green cabbage, sliced thinly**
- **2 medium apples (300g), julienned**
- **1 large fennel bulb (550g), sliced thinly (see tip)**
- **1 cup (250ml) creamy ranch dressing (see page 107)**
- **½ cup fresh mint leaves**

1 Preheat oven to 200°C/400°F.

2 Combine sauces, vinegar, paprika, garlic salt and chilli. Place ribs in a large roasting pan. Pour over marinade; turn to coat. Cover tightly with foil; roast for 30 minutes.

3 Meanwhile, remove husks from corn, keeping ends intact of you like; spread butter over corn. Place on an oven tray, season.

4 Remove foil from ribs, return to oven with corn. Roast, turning once halfway through cooking, brushing ribs all over with marinade, for a further 25 minutes or until pork is sticky and meat is tender. Meanwhile, roast corn for remaining 25 minutes of pork cooking time or until cooked through.

5 Make apple slaw.

6 Serve ribs with apple slaw and corn.

APPLE SLAW Combine cabbage, apple, fennel and dressing in a large bowl; season to taste. Add mint just before serving; stir gently to combine.

tips If your family aren't fennel fans, swap the fennel with 1 cup thinly sliced red cabbage and a grated carrot. Sprinkle with small mint leaves before serving, if you like. You will need about ¼ cabbage for the apple slaw.

even faster You could halve the marinade and use to marinate 800g pork fillets instead, then roast for 25 minutes or until tender and just cooked through. Instead of cutting the cabbage and fennel, add the sliced apple to a packet of purchased coleslaw mix instead. Use a good quality purchased ranch dressing instead of making your own.

do ahead If time permits, marinate the ribs, covered, for up to 24 hours ahead in the fridge.

FETTA & SPINACH-STUFFED LAMB
WITH ROASTED VEG

PREP + COOK TIME 50 MINUTES (+ STANDING) **SERVES** 4

- ⅓ cup (80ml) olive oil
- 1½ teaspoons ground cumin
- 1 tablespoon toasted sesame seeds
- 2 tablespoons honey
- 1 small cauliflower (1kg), trimmed, cut into florets
- 2 small orange sweet potato (500g), cut into wedges
- 250g (8oz) small brussels sprouts
- ⅓ cup (50g) coarsely chopped pitted kalamata olives
- 100g (3oz) fetta, crumbled
- 40g (1½oz) baby spinach, chopped coarsely
- 2 mini lamb roasts (700g)
- 2 tablespoons fresh coriander (cilantro) leaves
- 2 tablespoons fresh mint leaves
- 1 quantity mint sauce (see page 179), to serve

1 Preheat oven to 210°C/410°F. Line an oven tray with baking paper.

2 Combine oil, cumin, 2 teaspoons of the sesame seeds and honey in a large bowl; season. Add cauliflower, sweet potato and brussels sprouts; toss to combine. Place vegetable mixture on tray.

3 Combine olives, fetta and spinach in a medium bowl. Cut a horizontal pocket in each roast; do not cut all the way through. Press half the fetta mixture into each pocket; wrap with kitchen string to form a compact shape (or secure with toothpicks).

4 Heat an oiled small ovenproof frying pan over high heat. Cook lamb roasts, turning, for 10 minutes or until browned all over.

5 Transfer vegetables and lamb roasts to oven; roast for 20 minutes or until lamb is cooked as desired, and vegetables are golden and tender. Stand lamb, loosely covered with foil, for 10 minutes.

6 Cut lamb into thick slices; sprinkle with coriander, mint and remaining sesame seeds. Serve with roasted vegetables and mint sauce, if you like.

tips While the lamb is best stuffed just before roasting, you can prepare the fetta filling up to 4 hours ahead of time and store, covered, in the fridge. Swap 170g (5½oz) trimmed asparagus for brussels sprouts, if you prefer.

CREAMY
MUSHROOM SAUCE

PREP + COOK TIME
15 MINUTES **SERVES** 4

Melt 40g (1½oz) butter in a heavy-
based frying pan over medium–high
heat; cook 400g (12½oz) sliced
button mushrooms, stirring, until
browned. Add 1 crushed clove garlic;
stir for 1 minute. Stir in ¾ cup beef
stock and ¾ cup pouring cream;
simmer until thickened slightly. Stir in
2 tablespoons finely chopped fresh
flat-leaf parsley. Season to taste.

SAGE & ONION GRAVY

PREP + COOK TIME
20 MINUTES **SERVES** 4

Heat 2 tablespoons olive oil in a medium
saucepan over medium–high heat; cook
1 small clove crushed garlic and ½ cup
caramelised onion for 1 minute or until
fragrant. Add 1 tablespoon plain flour;
cook, stirring, for 1 minute. Gradually
add 1 cup chicken or beef stock, then
8 torn sage leaves and ⅓ cup cider;
simmer for 10 minutes or until gravy is
thickened slightly. Season to taste.

SAUCES & GRAVY

MINT SAUCE

PREP + COOK TIME
10 MINUTES (+ STANDING)
MAKES 1 CUP

Place 1 cup firmly packed fresh mint leaves in a heatproof bowl. Stir ¼ cup water, ¾ cup white wine vinegar and 2 tablespoons white sugar in a heavy-based saucepan over low heat, without boiling, until sugar dissolves; pour over mint. Cover; stand 3 hours. Strain liquid into a jug; discard mint. Add 1 cup firmly packed fresh mint leaves to liquid; blend or process until chopped finely.

MANGO CHUTNEY YOGHURT

PREP + COOK TIME 5 MINUTES
MAKES 1¼ CUPS

Combine 1 cup (280g) Greek-style yoghurt and 2 teaspoons lemon juice in a small bowl; season to taste. Swirl through 2 tablespoons mango chutney. Season with freshly ground pepper and top with coriander (cilantro) leaves before serving, if you like.

A HOME-MADE SAUCE CAN BE THAT LITTLE EXTRA TOUCH THAT ELEVATES A MEAL FROM BEING ORDINARY TO EXTRAORDINARY. OUR RECIPES INVOLVE ONLY A LITTLE PREPARATION BUT THE RESULTS ARE FULL OF FRESH FLAVOURS AND ARE SURE TO MAKE DINNER SOMETHING SPECIAL

FRAGRANT FISH & GREEN TEA
NOODLE PARCELS

PREP + COOK TIME 50 MINUTES **SERVES** 4

- **125g (4oz) butter, softened**
- **2 cloves garlic, crushed**
- **½ cup finely chopped fresh coriander (cilantro) leaves**
- **2 teaspoons fish sauce**
- **2 fresh kaffir lime leaves, chopped finely**
- **150g (4½oz) green tea soba noodles**

- **1 bunch gai lan (500g), trimmed, cut into 10cm (4in) lengths**
- **100g (3oz) fresh shiitake mushrooms, sliced thinly**
- **4 x 150g (4½oz) firm skinless boneless white fish fillets (see tip)**
- **100g (3oz) snow peas, shredded**

1 Preheat oven to 180°C/350°F.

2 Combine butter, garlic, coriander, fish sauce and lime leaf in a small bowl. Place on a sheet of baking paper; form into a log shape. Roll up, twisting ends; place in freezer to firm.

3 Meanwhile, cook noodles in a large saucepan of boiling water for 2 minutes or until tender; drain well. Cut thick gai lan stems in half lengthways.

4 Place four 50cm-long foil sheets on a work surface. Top with each with a sheet of baking paper. Divide noodles evenly among sheets; top evenly with gai lan, mushrooms, fish and snow peas. Cut butter into 1cm (½in) thick slices. Arrange half slices over fish; season. Wrap up parcels securely to enclose vegetables and fish, folding in sides.

5 Place parcels on a large oven tray; bake for 20 minutes or until fish is cooked through.

6 Open fish parcels; top evenly with remaining butter slices. Serve topped with thinly sliced seeded fresh long red chilli and julienned green onion, if you like..

tip We used four even-sized blue-eye trevalla fillets, but you could use snapper, ling or barramundi.

OVEN-BAKED FISH CUTLETS, CIRCA 1988

To give this recipe an update we started with the classic flavouring combination of butter and citrus, but instead of sliced lime or lemon, opted for kaffir lime leaves combined with coriander and a splash of fish sauce. The fragrant green tea noodles and mixed vegetables replace the chips, making this a quick and easy meal-in-a-bag.

180

MODERN ROASTS

ROAST BEEF *BOURGUIGNON*

PREP + COOK TIME 1 HOUR 35 MINUTES (+ STANDING) **SERVES** 4

- **20g (¾oz) dried porcini mushrooms (optional, see tips)**
- **½ cup (125ml) water, boiling**
- **1kg (2lb) piece beef rump cap**
- **2 tablespoons olive oil**
- **800g (1½lb) baby (dutch) carrots, trimmed, halved lengthways**
- **12 pickling onions (360g), peeled, halved**
- **1 medium bulb garlic, separated into cloves, unpeeled**
- **200g (6½oz) mixed mushrooms (see tips)**
- **¼ cup (70g) tomato paste**
- **½ cup (125ml) red wine**
- **1 cup (250ml) beef stock**
- **4 sprigs fresh thyme, leaves picked, any flowers reserved**

1 Preheat oven to 180°C/350°F. Place porcini and the boiling water in a small heatproof bowl; stand to infuse.

2 Meanwhile, using a sharp knife, score beef fat crossways at 5mm (¼in) intervals. Rub beef all over with oil; season generously. Heat a large flameproof roasting pan over high heat; cook beef, fat-side down, for 6 minutes or until browned. Cook beef, turning, for a further 4 minutes or until browned on all sides.

3 Arrange carrot, onion and garlic in centre of same roasting pan; top with beef, fat-side up. Roast for 45 minutes for medium–rare or until cooked to your liking. Transfer vegetables to a large plate, squeeze garlic from skins, reserve seperately. Transfer beef to a tray, cover loosely with foil; stand.

4 Meanwhile, heat same roasting pan over high heat; cook mixed mushrooms, stirring, for 6 minutes or until golden. Season to taste; transfer to plate with other vegetables.

5 Reduce heat to medium, add tomato paste; cook, stirring for 1 minute. Add red wine, stir to deglaze; cook for a further 1 minute. Add rehydrated porcinis and strained soaking liquid (if using), beef stock and thyme leaves; bring to the boil. Add garlic, reduce heat to medium; simmer for 20 minutes or until sauce is reduced and thickened. Strain sauce into a jug, pressing on garlic and herbs to extract as much liquid as possible.

6 Serve sliced roast beef with mushrooms, carrots and onions, drizzled with sauce and sprinkled with thyme flowers, if you like.

tips Swap porcini mushrooms with dried shiitake mushrooms and use all swiss brown mushrooms instead of a mixture, if you prefer. Slice or halve the mushrooms, if large. Store leftover roast beef in the fridge for up to 3 days and use in salads or sandwiches.

NUT–CRUMBED LAMB RACKS
WITH HASSELBACK ROAST VEG

PREP + COOK TIME 1 HOUR 15 MINUTES (+ STANDING) **SERVES** 4

- **4 cloves garlic, sliced thinly**
- **⅓ cup fresh rosemary leaves**
- **¼ cup (20g) panko (japanese) breadcrumbs**
- **½ cup (70g) unsalted macadamias, roasted, chopped coarsely**
- **½ cup (70g) hazelnuts, roasted, chopped coarsely**
- **⅓ cup (80ml) extra virgin olive oil**

- **400g (12½oz) small purple potatoes (see tip)**
- **400g (12½oz) celeriac (celery root), peeled, cut into 4cm (1½in) wedges**
- **1 large orange sweet potato (500g), halved lengthways, cut into 4cm (1½in) thick slices**
- **1kg (2lb) whole french–trimmed lamb rack, fat trimmed, cut into sections of 3 cutlets**
- **2 tablespoons dijon mustard**

1 Preheat oven to 180°C/350°F.

2 Process 1 clove of the garlic, 2 tablespoons rosemary, the breadcrumbs, macadamias and hazelnuts until coarsely chopped and just combined. Place in a small bowl with 2 tablespoons of the oil; stir to combine.

3 Cut horizontal slits, 1mm (⅛in) apart, in each vegetable, cutting halfway through (take care not to cut all the way through).

4 Toss vegetables with remaining rosemary and garlic, making sure some get stuck inside vegetable cuts; season. Coat vegetables in remaining oil; place in one layer in a large roasting pan. Roast, turning once, for 30 minutes or until crisp and golden.

5 Meanwhile, brush lamb racks evenly with mustard; season well. Pat nut mixture evenly and firmly onto lamb; place in a large roasting pan. Increase oven temperature to 200°C/400°F. Roast lamb alongside vegetables for 15 minutes or until lamb is browned. Reduce oven to 190°C/375°F; roast for a further 20 minutes for medium–rare or continue until cooked as desired. Cover lamb loosely with foil; rest for 10 minutes.

6 Serve lamb with roasted vegetables; season to taste.

tip If purple potatoes are unavailable, use baby (new) potatoes instead.

serving suggestion Serve with mint sauce (see page 179) spooned over the lamb and roast vegetables, if you like, and steamed green beans or broccolini alongside, sprinkled with small mint leaves.

MISO-ROASTED WHOLE CAULIFLOWER
WITH SPRING VEG SALAD

PREP + COOK TIME 45 MINUTES **SERVES** 4

- **1.3kg (2¾lb) whole cauliflower**
- **1 cup (250ml) dry sherry**
- **¼ cup (65g) white (shiro) miso paste**
- **¼ cup (60ml) pure maple syrup**
- **2 tablespoons olive oil**
- **1 tablespoon finely grated fresh ginger**
- **2 cloves garlic, crushed**
- **1 tablespoon sesame seeds**

SPRING VEG SALAD

- **3 teaspoons brazil and cashew nut spread**
- **1 tablespoon white miso (shiro) paste**
- **1 tablespoon mirin**
- **2 teaspoons water**
- **1 tablespoon olive oil**
- **¼ teaspoon sesame oil**
- **200g (6½oz) sugar snap peas, halved lengthways**
- **170g (5½oz) asparagus, cut into 4cm (1½in) lengths**
- **400g (12½oz) baby (dutch) carrots, trimmed, halved lengthways**
- **12 radishes (300g), trimmed, scrubbed, halved**
- **½ cup (75g) roasted cashews, chopped coarsely**

1 Preheat oven to 200°C/400°F.

2 Cut a cross in base of cauliflower with a sharp knife. Place cauliflower in a large, cast-iron casserole dish or deep roasting pan. Pour sherry into base of dish.

3 Combine miso, maple syrup, oil, ginger and garlic in a small bowl; season. Spread over cauliflower. Cover dish with lid or foil; roast for 20 minutes. Sprinkle cauliflower with half of the sesame seeds; roast for a further 15 minutes or until cauliflower is tender and browned lightly.

4 Meanwhile, make spring veg salad.

5 Sprinkle cauliflower with remaining sesame seeds; serve with spring veg salad. Sprinkle with micro radish leaves before serving, if you like.

SPRING VEG SALAD Place nut spread, miso, mirin, the water, olive oil and sesame oil in a small screw-top jar; shake well until smooth and combined. Boil, steam or microwave sugar snap peas and asparagus until tender; drain. Cover to keep warm. Place all vegetables, cashews and dressing in a large bowl; toss to combine.

tips If you don't have space in your oven to cook a whole cauliflower, cut it into six wedges and lay them flat in a roasting pan, then bake for 15 minutes; alternatively, use six baby cauliflowers for individual serves. White (shiro) miso is sweeter and milder in taste than brown, red and black miso, making it perfect for dressings. It is available from most major supermarkets and Asian food stores. Use regular radishes, if you prefer.

INDIAN-SPICED ROAST BEEF
& ROOT VEGETABLES

PREP + COOK TIME 1 HOUR 20 MINUTES (+ STANDING) **SERVES** 6

- 3 teaspoons ground cumin
- 2 teaspoons ground coriander
- 2 teaspoons ground turmeric
- 2 teaspoons garam masala
- 2 cloves garlic, crushed
- 2cm (¾in) piece fresh ginger, peeled, grated finely
- 2 teaspoons brown sugar
- 1kg (2lb) piece beef eye-fillet
- 2 tablespoons olive oil
- ⅓ cup fresh coriander (cilantro) leaves
- 1 quantity mango chutney yoghurt (see page 179), to serve

SPICE-ROASTED ROOT VEGETABLES
- 800g (1½lb) baby (dutch) carrots, trimmed, peeled
- 6 medium parsnips (1.5kg), peeled, quartered
- 2 bunches baby beetroots (beets) (1kg), peeled, quartered
- 12 cloves garlic, peeled
- 3 teaspoons garam masala
- 2 tablespoons olive oil

1 Preheat oven to 200°C /400°F.

2 Mix spices, garlic, ginger and sugar in a small bowl to make a paste; season.

3 Tie beef with kitchen string at 4cm (1½in) intervals. Rub beef all over with spice paste. Cover; stand for 20 minutes for flavours to develop.

4 Meanwhile, make spice-roasted root vegetables.

5 Heat oil in a large heavy-based frying pan over high heat; cook beef for 8 minutes, turning until browned all over. Add browned beef to pan with vegetables; roast for a further 25 minutes for medium-rare or until beef is cooked as desired. Transfer beef to a plate; stand, covered loosely with foil, for 10 minutes.

6 Cut beef into slices; top beef and roasted vegetables with coriander. Drizzle with a little of the mango chutney yoghurt and serve with remaining yoghurt.

SPICE-ROASTED ROOT VEGETABLES Line a roasting pan with baking paper. Combine ingredients in a large bowl; season. Place vegetable mixture in pan in a single layer; roast for 15 minutes.

even faster Instead of using the combined spices in step 2, use 2 tablespoons of your favourite curry powder.

FAST MOROCCAN ROAST LAMB
WITH BUTTER BEAN HUMMUS

PREP + COOK TIME 40 MINUTES (+ REFRIGERATION) **SERVES** 4

- 350g (11oz) mini vine sweet capsicums (bell peppers) (see tips)
- 8 zucchini flowers (160g) (see tips)
- 4 yellow squash (120g)
- 1 clove garlic, crushed
- 2 tablespoons olive oil
- 2 lamb backstraps (eye of loin) (400g)
- 2 teaspoons cumin seeds
- 2 teaspoons sumac
- lemon wedges, to serve

BUTTER BEAN HUMMUS
- 800g (1½lb) canned butter beans, drained, rinsed
- 100ml warm water
- ¼ cup (70g) hulled tahini
- ¼ cup (70g) Greek-style yoghurt
- 2 tablespoons lemon juice
- 2 cloves garlic, crushed
- 3 teaspoons ground cumin

1 Preheat oven to 240°C/475°F.

2 Combine capsicum, zucchini, squash, garlic and 1 tablespoon of the oil in a roasting pan; season. Roast for 15 minutes.

3 Combine lamb, cumin, sumac and remaining oil in a medium bowl; season.

4 Add lamb to roasting pan with vegetables; roast for 10 minutes for medium–rare or until lamb is cooked as desired. Remove lamb from pan, cover; rest for 5 minutes.

5 Meanwhile, make butter bean hummus.

6 Slice lamb thinly; serve with vegetables, hummus and lemon wedges.

BUTTER BEAN HUMMUS Blend or process ingredients until smooth; season to taste. (Makes 3 cups)

tips Swap 3 medium red capsicums, cut into thick slices and 3 small zucchini for the mini capsicums and zucchini flowers, if you prefer. Roast double the quantity of lamb, if you like, so there is plenty leftover to use with any leftover hummus to fill lunch-time wraps the next day. Use canned cannellini beans in the hummus instead of butter beans, if you prefer.

even faster Instead of making the hummus, serve with store-bought hummus.

serving suggestion Serve with grilled flatbread. Sprinkle with micro mint before serving, if you like.

do ahead The butter bean hummus can be made up to 3 days in advance; store in an airtight container in the fridge.

ROAST LAMB SHAWARMA
WITH WARM CARROT SALAD

PREP + COOK TIME 3 HOURS 25 MINUTES **SERVES** 4

- ½ cup (125ml) olive oil
- 2 tablespoons dukkah
- 4 cloves garlic, crushed
- 1 tablespoon finely grated lemon rind
- 2kg (4lb) piece butterflied lamb leg
- 3 cups (750ml) beef stock
- ¼ cup (75g) pomegranate molasses
- ¼ cup (60ml) water
- 800g (1½lb) mixed baby (dutch) carrots , trimmed, scrubbed
- 2 tablespoons lemon juice
- 4 large Greek-style pitta breads (320g)
- fresh flat-leaf parsley and mint leaves, to serve

1 Preheat oven to 180°C/350°F.

2 Preheat a grill plate (or barbecue) over high heat. Place half of the oil, the dukkah, garlic and lemon rind in a small bowl; stir to form a paste. Rub all over lamb; season generously.

3 Cook lamb leg in an oiled flameproof roasting pan for 6 minutes on each side or until browned all over; add beef stock to pan. Cover tightly with foil. Roast for 3 hours or until meat is tender and falling apart; removing foil for last 20 minutes of cooking time.

4 Transfer lamb leg to an oven tray, cover loosely with foil; stand for 15 minutes. Add pomegranate molasses and the water to pan juices. Bring sauce to a simmer over medium-high heat; cook, stirring, for 10 minutes or until reduced to a syrup consistency.

5 Meanwhile, bring a large saucepan of salted water to the boil. Blanch baby carrots for 2 minutes. Place lemon juice and remaining olive oil in a small bowl; whisk until thick and emulsified. Drain carrots, toss with dressing; season to taste.

6 Grill pitta bread on a grill plate (or pan or barbecue) over medium heat until warmed through and charred; cut into wedges. Shred lamb with two forks, discarding fat; toss through pomegranate sauce.

7 Top shredded lamb and carrot salad with herbs; serve with pitta bread. Seaon to taste.

serving suggestion Serve with your favourite store-bought hummus, baba ganoush or raita or make the butter bean hummus on page 191. Sprinkle with pomegranate seeds, if you like.

CARROTS FETTA
RISONI
SESAME
Lamb
PUMPKIN
PRAWNS
YOGHURT
EGGS *Paneer*
CORIANDER
MUSHROOMS
Za'atar
QUINOA

Dinner IN A DISH

SUPER-GREEN VEGETABLE CURRY

PREP + COOK TIME 55 MINUTES **SERVES** 4

- ½ cup (125ml) grapeseed oil
- 4 cloves garlic
- 1 cup fresh basil leaves
- 5cm (2in) piece fresh ginger, chopped finely
- 1 fresh long green chilli, seeded, sliced thinly
- 1 bunch fresh coriander (cilantro), stalks and roots reserved
- 200g (6½oz) kale, washed, sliced
- 120g (4oz) baby spinach leaves
- 600g (1¼lb) lebanese eggplants, cut into 1.5cm (¾in) slices
- 670ml canned coconut milk, shaken well
- 2 cups (500ml) vegetable stock
- 1 cup (200g) pearl barley, rinsed
- 150g (4½oz) green beans
- 1 cup (120g) frozen peas, thawed
- 150g (4½oz) sugar snap peas
- lime wedges, to serve

1 Process half the oil, the garlic, basil, ginger, chilli, coriander stalks and roots, half the kale and half the spinach until a smooth paste forms; reserve ¼ cup paste.

2 Heat remaining oil in a large heavy-based saucepan over high heat; cook eggplant, in batches, for 3 minutes on each side or until golden and softened. Drain on paper towel.

3 Reduce heat to medium, add green paste; cook, stirring, for 1 minute or until fragrant. Add coconut milk, stock and barley; stir to combine. Cook, covered, for 20 minutes or until barley is just tender.

4 Stir in beans, peas, remaining kale and spinach, and green paste; cook for 3 minutes or until beans are just tender and barley is soft.

5 Top with coriander leaves, season to taste. Serve with lime wedges.

serving suggestion Serve curry with steamed basmati rice and topped with toasted flaked coconut.

SPICY VEGETABLE CURRY, CIRCA 1992

To give this recipe an update we made our own quick green curry paste, then used it as the base for cooking loads of green vegetables, including a healthy amount of the leafy green superstar, kale. The fresh flavours of coriander, basil and ginger shine through, making this a much lighter, brighter take on its stodgy root vegetable-based counterpart.

MISO OCEAN TROUT *HOT POT*

PREP + COOK TIME 35 MINUTES **SERVES** 4

- 2 tablespoons grapeseed oil
- 2 shallots (50g), sliced thinly
- 2 cloves garlic, crushed
- 1 tablespoon finely chopped fresh ginger
- 4 x 150g (4½oz) skinless boneless ocean trout fillets (see tips)
- 2 tablespoons white (shiro) miso paste
- 1 tablespoon sesame oil
- 2 tablespoons light soy sauce
- 2 tablespoons rice wine vinegar
- 1 tablespoon finely grated palm sugar
- 1 litre (4 cups) vegetable stock
- 200g (6½oz) dried egg noodles
- 2 cups (160g) shredded wombok (napa cabbage)
- 1 bunch baby buk choy (400g), halved
- 2 tablespoons lime juice
- 1 cup fresh coriander (cilantro) leaves
- 4 green onions (scallions), sliced thinly
- 1 fresh long red chilli, sliced (optional)
- lime wedges, to serve

1 Heat grapeseed oil in a large heavy-based saucepan over low heat; cook shallot, garlic and ginger for 2 minutes or until softened and fragrant.

2 Rub each trout fillet with 2 teaspoons miso paste. Increase heat to medium; add trout fillets to pan, cook, for 1 minute on each side or until browned slightly. Add sesame oil, soy sauce, vinegar and palm sugar; cook for a further 1 minute.

3 Add stock; bring to a simmer over high heat. Cook, covered, for 5 minutes. Add noodles; cook for 1 minute. Add wombok and buk choy; cook, covered, for a further 2 minutes or until noodles are just soft and vegetables start to wilt slightly. Stir in lime juice.

4 Top hotpot with coriander leaves, green onion and chilli; serve with lime wedges.

tip For best results, use even-sized thick ocean trout fillets from the middle of belly, or you could use salmon fillets, if you prefer.

veg instead To make this vegetarian, omit the ocean trout and replace with the same amount of firm tofu, cut into 2 cm cubes.

LAMB & MINT MEATBALLS *WITH RISONI*

PREP + COOK TIME 50 MINUTES **SERVES** 4

- **500g (1lb) minced (ground) lamb**
- **1 cup (70g) stale breadcrumbs**
- **¼ cup chopped fresh mint**
- **1 egg, beaten lightly**
- **1 medium onion (150g), grated**
- **2 cloves garlic, crushed**
- **1 medium lemon (140g), rind grated finely**
- **¼ cup (60ml) olive oil**
- **1 large eggplant (500g), diced**
- **1½ cups (330g) risoni pasta**
- **700g (1½lb) bottled tomato passata**
- **1½ cups (375ml) chicken stock**
- **125g (4oz) fetta, crumbled**
- **fresh small mint leaves and lemon wedges, to serve**

1 Combine lamb, breadcrumbs, chopped mint, egg, onion, garlic and half of the rind in a medium bowl; season well. Roll ¼ cup measures of mixture into balls.

2 Heat half the oil in a large heavy-based frying pan; cook meatballs, shaking pan occasionally, until browned all over. Remove from pan with a slotted spoon.

3 Heat remaining oil in same pan over medium-high heat; cook eggplant for 4 minutes or until golden brown.

4 Return meatballs to pan with risoni, passata and stock; stir to combine. Bring to the boil. Reduce heat to low; simmer, covered, stirring frequently, for 15 minutes or until meatballs are cooked through and risoni is tender.

5 Serve meatball mixture topped with fetta, remaining rind, extra mint leaves and lemon wedges. Season to taste.

tips The risoni mixture will thicken on standing; if it's too thick, add a little boiling water to loosen. If your family aren't eggplant fans, use 1 coarsely chopped large red capsicum (bell pepper) instead.

do ahead Uncooked meatballs can be frozen in an airtight container for up to 3 months.

PRAWN, ASPARAGUS & PEA
QUINOA RISOTTO

PREP + COOK TIME 50 MINUTES **SERVES** 4

- **600g (1¼lb) uncooked medium king prawns (shrimp)**
- **1 litre (4 cups) chicken stock**
- **1½ cups (375ml) water**
- **30g (1oz) butter**
- **1½ tablespoons olive oil**
- **1 small onion (80g), chopped finely**
- **1 cup (200g) quinoa, rinsed**
- **2 cloves garlic, crushed**
- **500g (1lb) asparagus, trimmed, cut into 4cm (1½) lengths**
- **1½ cups (180g) frozen peas**
- **1 teaspoon finely grated lemon rind**
- **½ cup (40g) finely grated parmesan**
- **lemon wedges, to serve**

1 Shell and devein prawns, leaving tails intact.

2 Place stock and the water in a large saucepan; bring to the boil. Reduce heat to low; simmer, covered.

3 Meanwhile, heat half the butter and 1 tablespoon of the oil in a large heavy-based saucepan; cook onion, stirring, for 3 minutes or until soft. Add quinoa; stir to coat quinoa in onion mixture. Add all the stock mixture, bring to the boil, reduce heat to low; cook for 20 minutes or until liquid is absorbed and quinoa is tender.

4 Meanwhile, heat remaining butter and oil in a medium frying pan over medium heat; cook prawns and garlic, stirring, for 2 minutes or until prawns change colour and are just cooked through. Season to taste.

5 Boil, steam or microwave asparagus and peas until just tender; drain.

6 Add asparagus, peas, prawn mixture, lemon rind and ⅓ cup of the parmesan to risotto; cook over low heat, stirring, until cheese melts.

7 Top risotto with remaining parmesan; serve with lemon wedges. Season with pepper.

tips If your family are not fans of asparagus, use sugar snap peas, snow peas or sliced green beans instead. Serve risotto topped with snow pea sprouts and mustard cress, if you like.

even faster To cut the time required to shell and devein the prawns, you can use 300g (9½oz) marinara mix instead.

veg instead To make this vegetarian, omit the prawns and use vegetable stock instead of chicken stock, then stir in a 400g (12½oz) drained and rinsed canned borlotti beans or ¾ cup (90g) podded blanched broad (fava) beans in step 6, stirring until warmed through.

HEALTHY **BUTTER CHICKEN**

PREP + COOK TIME 1 HOUR 5 MINUTES (+ STANDING & REFRIGERATION) **SERVES** 4

- 1 cup (150g) raw cashews,
  plus extra to serve
- 6 chicken drumsticks (900g) (see tip)
- 600ml buttermilk
- 2 tablespoons turmeric
- 1 tablespoon ground cumin
- 1 tablespoon ground cinnamon
- 1 tablespoon ground coriander
- 1 tablespoon sweet paprika
- ¾ teaspoon ground cloves
- 1 tablespoon olive oil
- 1 large onion (200g),
  chopped coarsely
- 2 tablespoons tomato paste
- 1 medium orange sweet potato
  (400g), cut into 2cm (¾in) rounds
- 1 medium swede (225g), cut into
  2cm (¾in) wedges
- 3 cups (750ml) chicken stock
- 2 trimmed, cleaned corn cobs (500g),
  cut into 2cm (¾in) rounds
- 60g (2oz) watercress sprigs

1 Place cashews in a medium bowl, cover with cold water; stand for 30 minutes or until plump and pale in colour.

2 Meanwhile, place chicken, buttermilk and spices in a large bowl; stir well to coat chicken completely. Cover; refrigerate for 30 minutes.

3 Drain chicken; reserve marinade. Heat oil in a large heavy-based saucepan over high heat; cook chicken for 2 minutes on each side or until fragrant.

4 Add onion to pan; cook, stirring, for 2 minutes or until starting to become soft. Stir in tomato paste and reserved marinade; cook for 2 minutes or until mixture comes to a simmer and is fragrant.

5 Add sweet potato, swede and stock to pan; stir to combine. Bring to the boil, reduce heat to low; cook, covered, for 35 minutes or until chicken is falling off the bone and vegetables are tender when a small knife is inserted. Add corn during last 10 minutes of cooking time.

6 Meanwhile, drain cashews; reserve ½ cup of soaking liquid. Process cashews and reserved liquid until a smooth paste forms (use a high-powered blender, if you have one, this will achieve a very smooth result).

7 Stir in cashew paste until well combined to thicken sauce; cook, uncovered, for a further 5 minutes or until sauce thickens and coats the back of a wooden spoon. Season to taste.

8 Serve butter chicken topped with watercress; sprinkled with extra cashews.

tip Chicken lovely legs or thigh fillets can be used instead of drumsticks, if you prefer.
serving suggestion Serve with warmed naan and steamed basmati rice.

MEXICAN PULLED BEEF

PREP + COOK TIME 2 HOURS 35 MINUTES **SERVES** 6

- 2 tablespoons olive oil
- 1.2kg (2½lb) piece beef chuck steak, cut into 7cm (2¾in) chunks
- 1 medium onion (150g), chopped coarsely
- 4 cloves garlic, chopped coarsely
- 1 tablespoon mexican chilli powder
- 1 tablespoon smoked paprika
- ¾ cup (180ml) freshly squeezed orange juice
- 400g (12½oz) canned diced tomatoes
- 2 cups (500ml) beef stock
- 12 wholegrain mini tortillas (300g), warmed
- 2 medium avocados (500g), sliced
- 400g (12½oz) mixed cherry tomatoes, halved (see tips)
- 250g (8oz) light sour cream
- fresh coriander (cilantro) sprigs and lime wedges, to serve

1 Heat a flameproof casserole dish over high heat and add 1 tablespoon oil; cook half the beef for 2 minutes on each side or until browned. Transfer to a plate. Repeat with remaining beef.

2 Reduce heat to medium, add remaining oil, the onion and garlic; cook for 5 minutes or until softened. Add spices; cook for 2 minutes or until fragrant.

3 Add orange juice, scraping the bottom of the dish; bring to the boil over high heat. Add tomatoes, stock and beef, stirring until well combined; bring to the boil. Season.

4 Cover dish with a tight-fitting lid; reduce heat to low. Cook for 1½ hours. Remove lid; simmer, uncovered, for a further 30 minutes or until meat is tender enough to shred. Shred beef in dish using two forks; simmer, stirring, over high heat for 10 minutes or until sauce is reduced and thickened.

5 Divide pulled beef among tortillas, top with avocado, tomatoes, sour cream, coriander and lime wedges.

tips You can cook the beef in a preheated 180°C/350°F oven for 2 hours, for 6 hours in a slow cooker, or 25 minutes in a pressure cooker. Different brands of chilli powder may differ in flavour and heat levels, so adjust the amount to your liking. We used heirloom cherry tomatoes here, however regular cherry tomatoes can be used instead. For those who like it extra spicy, serve with smoky chipotle Tabasco sauce.

do ahead The recipe can be prepared to the end of step 4 up to 3 days ahead; refrigerate in an airtight container. Reheat just before serving. Leftovers can be frozen in an airtight container for up to 3 months.

SPICED LAMB PILAF
WITH ALMONDS & CURRANTS

PREP + COOK TIME 35 MINUTES (+ STANDING) **SERVES** 4

- 600g (1¼lb) lamb tenderloin fillets
- 1 tablespoon ground cumin
- ¼ cup (60ml) olive oil
- 1 medium red onion (170g), chopped finely
- 1 medium red capsicum (bell pepper) (200g), chopped finely
- 1 stick cinnamon
- 1 teaspoon ground allspice
- 1 bunch fresh coriander (cilantro)
- 2 cups (400g) basmati rice
- 1 litre (4 cups) chicken stock
- ½ cup (80g) currants
- 2 medium carrots (240g), julienned
- ½ cup (70g) slivered almonds, toasted
- lemon wedges, to serve

1 Coat lamb in cumin. Heat a large flameproof casserole dish with a tight-fitting lid over high heat; add 1 tablespoon of the oil. Cook lamb, turning, for 4 minutes or until browned all over; transfer to a plate. Cover to keep warm.

2 Add remaining oil to dish, reduce heat to medium-high; cook onion and capsicum for 5 minutes or until softened and browned lightly. Add cinnamon stick and allspice; cook for 30 seconds. Remove leaves from coriander; reserve. Finely chop roots and stems; you will need ⅓ cup. Add to dish with rice, stirring to coat grains well.

3 Add stock and currant; bring to the boil. Reduce heat to low; cook, covered, for 10 minutes. Remove from heat; stand, covered, for 5 minutes. Discard cinnamon stick.

4 Slice lamb thickly on the diagonal; place on top of rice mixture with carrot, almonds and coriander leaves. Season to taste; serve with lemon wedges.

tips Serve with Greek-style yoghurt sprinkled with a little ground cumin, if you like. Swap lamb leg steaks for the tenderloin fillets, if you prefer.

PORK ADOBO

PREP + COOK TIME 55 MINUTES (+ STANDING) **SERVES** 6

- 800g (1½lb) pork fillets, sliced thickly across the grain
- ⅓ cup (80ml) apple cider vinegar
- ⅓ cup (80ml) light soy sauce
- 2 bay leaves
- 3 cloves garlic, crushed
- 5cm (2in) piece fresh ginger, grated finely
- 1 tablespoon vegetable oil
- 2 cups (500ml) beef stock

- 2 tablespoons oyster sauce
- 1 medium orange sweet potato (400g), sliced thickly
- 200g (6½oz) baby green beans, trimmed
- 1¼ cups (245g) white long-grain rice
- 1¾ cups (430ml) water
- 400g (12½oz) can black beans, drained, rinsed
- ½ cup coarsely chopped fresh coriander (cilantro)

1 Place pork, vinegar, soy sauce, bay leaves, garlic and ginger in a large bowl; season. Stir to coat; refrigerate for 30 minutes for flavours to develop.

2 Drain pork; reserve marinade. Heat oil in a flameproof casserole dish or large heavy-based saucepan over high heat; cook half the pork mixture, stirring, for 5 minutes or until browned all over. Transfer to a plate. Repeat with remaining pork mixture.

3 Add reserved marinade, beef stock and oyster sauce to pan; stir in sweet potato. Bring to the boil, reduce heat to medium; cook, covered, for 20 minutes or until pork and sweet potato are tender. Stir in green beans; cook, covered, for 2 minutes or until beans are just tender. Cook, uncovered, over high heat for 3 minutes or until sauce is thickened and glossy.

4 Meanwhile, place rice and the water in a heavy-based saucepan; bring to the boil. Reduce heat to low; cook, covered for 12 minutes or until water is absorbed and rice is tender. Stir in black beans and coriander.

5 Serve pork adobo with black bean rice.

tip Sprinkle with fresh coriander sprigs before serving, if you like.

do ahead Pork can be prepared to the end of step 1 the day before and marinated in the fridge overnight.

BEEF & PORCINI MUSHROOM STEW
WITH PARMESAN MASH

PREP + COOK TIME 1 HOUR 40 MINUTES **SERVES** 4

- **20g (¾oz) dried porcini mushrooms (see tips)**
- **1 litre (4 cups) beef stock**
- **2 tablespoons olive oil**
- **1.5kg (3lb) beef rump steak, trimmed, cut into 4cm (1½in) pieces**
- **1 large onion (200g), chopped coarsely**
- **2 cloves garlic, crushed**
- **2 tablespoons tomato paste**
- **400g (12½oz) canned cherry tomatoes**
- **1 bay leaf**
- **250g (8oz) button mushrooms, halved**
- **2 tablespoons coarsely chopped fresh flat-leaf parsley**

PARMESAN MASH
- **1kg (2lb) floury potatoes (see tips), peeled, cut into large pieces**
- **¾ cup (180ml) pouring cream**
- **75g (2½oz) butter, chopped**
- **1 cup (80g) finely grated parmesan**

1 Place porcini mushrooms and 1 cup of the stock in a small bowl; soak for 10 minutes. Drain; reserve stock. Chop mushrooms finely.

2 Heat oil in a large flameproof casserole or heavy-based saucepan over medium–high heat; cook beef, in batches, turning until browned all over. Transfer to a large bowl.

3 Cook onion and garlic in same dish, stirring, until softened. Return beef to dish with paste, tomatoes, bay leaf, porcini mushrooms, reserved stock and remaining stock; bring to the boil. Reduce heat to low; cook, covered, for 30 minutes. Add button mushrooms. Cook, uncovered and stirring occasionally, for a further 1 hour or until meat is tender; add a little extra water if the sauce becomes too thick. Season to taste.

4 Meanwhile, make parmesan mash.

5 Serve beef stew with parmesan mash, sprinkled with parsley.

PARMESAN MASH Boil potato in a saucepan of salted water until tender. Drain; leave for a few minutes to dry. Heat cream and butter in same pan over low–medium heat; add potato, mashing into cream mixture with a potato masher until a smooth consistency. Remove from heat; stir in parmesan until combined. Season to taste.

tips While the porcini mushrooms add a rich, mushroom flavour to the stew, they can be omitted if preferred or use dried shiitake mushrooms instead. You can mash the potato with a potato ricer; add pressed potatoes to the warm cream, then stir in the butter and parmesan. Never mash potatoes in a food processor, as they will be gluey. Serve with a sliced baguette, if you like.

do ahead You can prepare the stew up to the end of step 3, then refrigerate in an airtight container for up to 2 days and reheat while you prepare the mash, or freeze the stew for up to 1 month.

CHAR-GRILLED PEACH CHICKEN

PREP + COOK TIME 50 MINUTES (+ STANDING) **SERVES** 4

- **1.6kg (3¼lb) chicken**
- **1 tablespoon za'atar (see tips)**
- **400g (12½oz) can chickpeas (garbanzo beans), drained, rinsed**
- **¼ cup (60ml) olive oil**
- **¼ cup (60ml) peach nectar (see tips)**
- **2 tablespoons red wine vinegar**
- **2 celery stalks (300g), trimmed, sliced thinly**
- **¼ cup (40g) currants**
- **4 medium peaches (600g), halved, seeded (see tips)**
- **2 medium red onions (340g), cut into wedges**
- **60g (2oz) watercress sprigs**

1 Place chicken, breast-side down, on a clean chopping board. Using poultry shears or sharp scissors, cut down either side of the backbone; discard (or freeze to make stock). Open chicken to lie flat. Turn, breast-side up; press firmly with the heel of your hand to flatten. Cut in half.

2 Preheat a grill plate (or pan or barbecue) over medium heat for 10 minutes.

3 Rub chicken all over with za'atar; season. Trim a piece of baking paper to fit grill plate. Cook chicken over medium heat for 25 minutes, turning carefully every 5 minutes with two tongs; cover chicken with a large roasting pan during cooking to ensure it cooks through. Transfer to a large plate, cover loosely with foil; leave to rest for 20 minutes.

4 Meanwhile, place chickpeas in a large bowl; lightly crush with a fork. Add 2 tablespoons of the oil, the nectar, vinegar, celery and currants; season. Stand for 20 minutes.

5 Brush peach halves and onion with remaining oil. Cook onion wedges for 5 minutes on grill plate, turning once. Cook peach halves, cut-side down, for 3 minutes or until char marks appear.

6 Add watercress to chickpea mixture; toss gently to mix.

7 Serve sliced chicken with chickpea salad, grilled peaches and onion.

tips If you don't have the Middle Eastern spice mix za'atar, combine 2 teaspoons dried rigani (greek oregano) or thyme, 2 teaspoons sesame seeds and ½ teaspoon sumac mixed with a pinch of sea salt. You can use apricots and apricot nectar instead of peaches and peach nectar for a new take on apricot chicken.

VEGETABLE TAGINE
WITH ZA'ATAR CHICKPEAS

PREP + COOK TIME 1 HOUR **SERVES** 4

- **2 teaspoons olive oil**
- **1 large red onion (300g), chopped coarsely**
- **2 cloves garlic, crushed**
- **4 baby eggplant (240g), halved lengthways**
- **500g (1lb) kent pumpkin, cut into 2cm (¾in) pieces**
- **2 teaspoons ground cumin**
- **2 teaspoons ground coriander**
- **2 teaspoons ground ginger**
- **½ teaspoon ground cinnamon**
- **400g (12½oz) canned cherry tomatoes (see tips)**
- **2 cups (500ml) vegetable stock**
- **300g (9½oz) baby zucchini, trimmed, halved lengthways**
- **¾ cup (200g) Greek-style yoghurt**
- **½ cup finely chopped fresh flat-leaf parsley**
- **½ cup finely chopped fresh mint**

ZA'ATAR CHICKPEAS

- **400g (12½oz) canned chickpeas (garbanzo beans), drained, rinsed**
- **1 tablespoon za'atar (see tips)**
- **1 tablespoon olive oil**

1 Make za'atar chickpeas.

2 Heat oil in a large heavy-based saucepan over medium heat; cook onion and garlic, stirring, for 5 minutes. Add eggplant and pumpkin; cook for 1 minute on each side or until vegetables are browned lightly. Add spices; cook for 1 minute or until fragrant. Add tomatoes and stock; bring to the boil. Reduce heat to low; simmer, covered for 15 minutes or until vegetables are just tender.

3 Meanwhile, boil, steam or microwave zucchini until tender; drain. Stir into tagine.

4 Place yoghurt and herbs in a small bowl; stir to combine. Season to taste.

5 Serve tagine topped with yoghurt mixture and za'atar chickpeas. Season with pepper. Sprinkle with small mint and flat-leaf parsley leaves, if you like.

ZA'ATAR CHICKPEAS Preheat oven to 200°C/400°F. Line a large oven tray with baking paper. Pat chickpeas dry with paper towel; place in a medium bowl. Add remaining ingredients to chickpeas; stir to combine. Season to taste. Spread chickpeas in a single layer on tray. Bake for 20 minutes, stirring three times during cooking, or until well browned and slightly crunchy.

tips Use a can of chopped tomatoes instead of canned cherry tomatoes, if you prefer. If you don't have the Middle Eastern spice mix za'atar, combine 2 teaspoons dried rigani (greek oregano) or thyme, 2 teaspoons sesame seeds and ½ teaspoon sumac mixed with a pinch of sea salt.

even faster Instead of making the za'atar chickpeas, add the drained, rinsed chickpeas directly to the tagine with the tomatoes in step 2.

serving suggestion Serve with the cauliflower 'rice' pilaf on page 63.

PREP + COOK TIME 20 MINUTES
SERVES 4

Place 1 cup quinoa and 2 cups water in a medium saucepan; bring to the boil. Reduce heat to low; cook, covered, for 12 minutes or until the water is absorbed and quinoa is tender. Stir in 1/3 cup toasted pine nuts, 2 teaspoons finely grated lemon rind, 2 tablespoons lemon juice and 1/2 cup finely chopped fresh flat–leaf parsley; season to taste.

POTATO **PUREE**

PREP + COOK TIME
30 MINUTES **SERVES** 4

Place 1kg (2lb) coarsely chopped peeled potatoes in a medium saucepan with enough cold water to barely cover the potato. Boil over medium heat for 15 minutes or until potato is tender; drain. Using the back of a wooden spoon, push potato through a fine sieve into a large bowl. Stir 40g (1½oz) butter and ¾ cup hot milk into potato, folding gently until mash is smooth and fluffy. Season to taste.

GRAINS & MASHES

SOFT *POLENTA*

PREP + COOK TIME
20 MINUTES **SERVES** 6

Combine 3 cups milk and 2 cups chicken stock in a large saucepan; bring to the boil. Gradually add 2 cups polenta to liquid, stirring constantly. Reduce heat; simmer, stirring, for 10 minutes or until polenta thickens. Add 1 cup milk and ¼ cup finely grated parmesan; stir until parmesan melts. Season to taste; top with extra grated parmesan, if you like.

LEMON PISTACHIO COUSCOUS

PREP + COOK TIME
15 MINUTES **SERVES** 4

Combine 1 cup couscous, ¾ cup boiling water, 2 teaspoons finely grated lemon rind and ¼ cup lemon juice in a medium heatproof bowl. Cover; stand for 5 minutes or until liquid is absorbed, fluffing with a fork occasionally. Meanwhile, cook ½ cup pistachios in a heated small dry frying pan until fragrant; chop coarsely. Heat 2 teaspoons olive oil in same pan, add 1 crushed garlic clove and 1 finely chopped small red onion; cook, stirring, until onion softens. Fluff the couscous then stir pistachios, onion mixture and ½ cup shredded fresh mint through couscous.

SKIP THE PLAIN WHITE RICE OR CRUSTY BREAD AND INSTEAD MAKE ONE OF THESE TASTY SIDES TO ACCOMPANY A RICH STEW OR SPICY CURRY. DON'T LET A SINGLE DROP OF SAUCE GO TO WASTE WITH THESE MASHES & GRAIN SALADS TO SOP UP ANY EXTRA TASTY JUICES.

AUTUMN CHICKEN FRICASEE
WITH BUTTERMILK SCONES

PREP + COOK TIME 1 HOUR 5 MINUTES **SERVES** 4

- 20g (¾oz) dried porcini mushrooms
- 1 cup (250ml) boiling water
- 1 tablespoon olive oil
- 4 chicken thigh fillets (680g), cut into thirds
- 1 large onion (200g), sliced thinly
- 2 cloves garlic, crushed
- 4 portobello mushrooms (200g), trimmed, sliced thickly
- 200g (6½oz) swiss brown mushrooms, quartered
- ½ cup (125ml) white wine (see tips)
- 2½ cups (625ml) chicken stock
- 400g (12½oz) kipfler (fingerling) potatoes, unpeeled, sliced thickly on the diagonal
- 1 tablespoon fresh thyme leaves
- 2 tablespoons coarsely chopped fresh sage

BUTTERMILK SCONES
- 2 cups (300g) self-raising flour
- ¼ teaspoon bicarbonate of soda (baking soda)
- 1 teaspoon sea salt flakes
- 60g (2oz) cold butter, chopped coarsely
- ¾ cup (180ml) buttermilk
- 1 tablespoon fresh thyme leaves
- 1 tablespoon finely chopped fresh sage
- 1 tablespoon finely chopped fresh flat-leaf parsley
- olive-oil spray

1 Place porcini mushrooms and the boiling water in a small bowl; stand.

2 Meanwhile, heat oil in a flameproof casserole dish or large heavy-based saucepan over high heat. Add chicken; cook for 3 minutes on each side or until golden and caramelised. Transfer to a plate.

3 Reduce heat to medium, add onion; cook, stirring, for 5 minutes or until softened. Add garlic, portobello and swiss brown mushrooms, drained porcini and strained reserved soaking liquid; cook, stirring, for 8 minutes or until mushrooms are softened. Add wine, bring to a simmer; cook for 5 minutes or until reduced slightly.

4 Return chicken to pan, add stock and potato; bring to the boil; reduce heat to low-medium. Cook, covered, for 25 minutes. Remove lid; cook for a further 10 minutes or until chicken and potato are tender and sauce reduces slightly.

5 Meanwhile, make buttermilk scones.

6 Sprinkle chicken fricasee with herbs; season to taste. Serve with buttermilk scones.

BUTTERMILK SCONES Preheat oven to 180°C/350°F. Grease and line a large oven tray with baking paper. Place flour, soda and salt in a medium bowl; rub in butter. Stir in buttermilk and herbs to make a soft, sticky dough. Place 12 spoonfuls of dough onto lined tray; spray lightly with oil. Bake for 15 minutes or until light golden and cooked through. Transfer to a wire rack to cool.

tips If you prefer, omit the white wine and replace with extra stock, so you use 2 cups (500ml) chicken stock in total instead and add all the stock at once in step 3. To cook this all in the same pan, place spoonfuls of the scone dough directly onto the stew; cook, covered, for 10 minutes, then uncovered for a further 8 minutes or until dumplings spring back when pressed lightly.

do ahead Prepare to the end of step 4 up to 2 days in advance, then refrigerate in an airtight container. Reheat in the same dish, then proceed with the recipe 30 minutes before you wish to serve.

CHAI-ROASTED PUMPKIN SOUP
WITH WHIPPED PANEER TOASTS

PREP + COOK TIME 50 MINUTES **SERVES** 4

- **2kg (4lb) butternut pumpkin, peeled, chopped coarsely**
- **1 teaspoon ground cardamom**
- **½ teaspoon cracked black pepper**
- **½ teaspoon ground cinnamon**
- **2 tablespoons olive oil**
- **1 medium onion (150g), chopped coarsely**
- **2 cloves garlic, sliced**
- **1½ cups (375ml) salt-reduced vegetable stock**
- **3 cups (750ml) water**
- **⅓ cup (95g) Greek-style yoghurt**
- **fresh coriander (cilantro) sprigs, to serve**

WHIPPED PANEER TOASTS

- **12 slices wholemeal sourdough bread**
- **⅓ cup (80ml) extra virgin olive oil**
- **200g (6½oz) paneer**
- **1 small clove garlic, crushed**
- **1 teaspoon lemon juice**

1 Preheat oven to 200°C/400°F. Line two large oven trays with baking paper.

2 Place pumpkin on trays, in a single layer; sprinkle with spices. Drizzle with 1 tablespoon of the oil; roast for 25 minutes or until tender.

3 Heat remaining oil in a large heavy-based saucepan over medium heat. Cook onion and garlic, stirring, for 5 minutes or until softened. Add pumpkin, stock and the water; bring to the boil. Remove from heat; cool for 10 minutes.

4 Meanwhile, make whipped paneer toasts.

5 Blend or process pumpkin mixture, in batches, until smooth. Return to pan; stir over medium heat until hot. Season to taste.

6 Divide soup among bowls, drizzle with yoghurt; season to taste. Sprinkle with coriander; serve with paneer toasts.

WHIPPED PANEER TOASTS Heat a grill pan (or plate) over medium heat. Brush bread with 2 tablespoons of the oil; grill for 1 minute on each side or until light char marks appear. Process paneer and garlic in a food processor, pulsing until mixture forms a spreadable consistency. With the motor operating, gradually add lemon juice, then remaining oil; process until light and fluffy. Spread whipped paneer onto toast. Season to taste.

tip You can use fetta instead of paneer, if you prefer.

do ahead You can freeze the soup in portion-sized airtight containers for up to 1 month.

223

PUMPKIN CREAM SOUP, CIRCA 1988

To give this recipe an update we replaced the familiar pumpkin soup stalwart, nutmeg, with the warming, chai-inspired mix of cardamom, pepper and cinnamon for an Indian-inspired take on this faithful classic. The whipped paneer toasts bring all the flavours together making this a hearty, substantial meal

CHICKEN WONTON NOODLE SOUP

PREP + COOK TIME 1 HOUR **SERVES** 4

- **2 teaspoons peanut oil**
- **2 cloves garlic, crushed**
- **2 litres (8 cups) chicken stock**
- **1 tablespoon japanese soy sauce**
- **1 litre (4 cups) water**
- **225g (7oz) fresh egg noodles**
- **800g (1½lb) baby buk choy, trimmed, halved or quartered lengthways**
- **4 fresh shiitake mushrooms, trimmed, sliced thinly**
- **4 green onions (scallions), sliced thinly**

CHICKEN WONTONS
- **150g (4½oz) minced (ground) chicken**
- **2 tablespoons finely chopped water chestnuts**
- **1 green onion (scallion), chopped finely**
- **1 clove garlic, chopped finely**
- **1 teaspoon finely grated fresh ginger**
- **1 teaspoon sesame oil**
- **1 teaspoon soy sauce**
- **16 wonton wrappers**

1 Make chicken wontons.

2 Heat oil in a large saucepan over low heat; cook garlic, stirring, for 2 minutes. Stir in stock, soy sauce and the water; bring to the boil. Reduce heat to low; simmer for 15 minutes. Season to taste.

3 Cook noodles in a saucepan of boiling water following the packet directions until tender; drain. Divide among bowls.

4 Add buk choy and mushrooms to soup; cook for 4 minutes or until buk choy is tender but still crisp. Add cooked wontons to soup to warm through. Divide wontons, vegetables and soup evenly among bowls.

5 Serve soup sprinkled with green onion; season to taste.

CHICKEN WONTONS Combine chicken, water chestnuts, green onion, garlic, ginger, oil and soy sauce in a bowl. Place 1 heaped teaspoon chicken mixture in centre of each wrapper. Brush edges with water; pinch edges together to seal. Cook wontons, in batches, in a large saucepan of simmering water for 4 minutes or until cooked through. Remove with a slotted spoon onto a large tray.

tips Use minced (ground) pork instead of minced chicken, if you prefer. Serve with chilli oil or your favourite chilli sauce, if you like. To save on washing up, add the wontons directly to the soup in step 4 to cook with the vegetables.

do ahead Uncooked wontons can be frozen in an airtight container, in single layers separated by sheets of baking paper, for up to 2 months.

HUNGARIAN GOULASH SOUP

PREP + COOK TIME 2 HOURS 45 MINUTES **SERVES** 4

- **2 tablespoons olive oil**
- **40g (1½oz) butter**
- **900g (1¾lb) boneless veal shoulder, chopped coarsely**
- **2 medium onions (300g), chopped finely**
- **1 tablespoon tomato paste**
- **1 tablespoon plain (all-purpose) flour**
- **1 tablespoon sweet paprika**
- **1 teaspoon caraway seeds**
- **½ teaspoon cayenne pepper**
- **2 cloves garlic, crushed**
- **2 cups (500ml) water**
- **1 litre (4 cups) beef stock**
- **400g (12½oz) canned chopped tomatoes**
- **1 large red capsicum (bell pepper) (350g), sliced thinly**
- **250g (8oz) potato gnocchi**

1 Heat half the oil and half the butter in a large heavy-based saucepan over medium-high heat; cook veal, in batches, for 5 minutes or until browned all over. Remove from pan.

2 Heat remaining oil and remaining butter in same pan over medium heat; cook onion, stirring, for 5 minutes or until softened.

3 Add paste, flour, paprika, caraway seeds, cayenne and garlic to pan; cook, stirring, for 2 minutes. Return veal to pan with the water, stock and tomatoes; bring to the boil. Reduce heat to low; simmer for 2½ hours. Add capsicum; cook for a further 10 minutes or until capsicum and beef are tender. Season to taste.

4 Meanwhile, cook gnocchi in a large saucepan of boiling water until gnocchi floats to the surface; drain.

5 Serve goulash soup with gnocchi.

tips You can swap beef chuck or blade steak for veal, if you like. This is a cross between a soup and a stew; if a thinner soup is preferred, cook for 1½ hours at step 3 and thin with boiling water or extra warmed stock to desired conistency. Serve soup sprinkled with fresh chervil, if you like.

do ahead Soup is suitable to freeze at the end of step 3. Thaw the soup in the fridge overnight; reheat and cook gnocchi just before serving.

VIETNAMESE BEEF & CARROT *HOT POT*

PREP + COOK TIME 45 MINUTES (+ REFRIGERATION) **SERVES** 4

- 600g (1¼lb) beef rump steak, fat trimmed, cut into 4cm (1½in) pieces
- 2 cloves garlic, chopped coarsely
- 5cm (2in) piece fresh ginger, peeled, julienned
- ½ teaspoon chinese five-spice powder
- ¼ cup (60ml) oyster sauce
- 2 tablespoons vegetable oil
- 1 litre (4 cups) beef stock
- 2 large carrots (360g), cut into 2cm (¾in) pieces
- 600g (1¼lb) kipfler (fingerling) potatoes, cut into 2cm (¾in) pieces
- 6 shallots (150g), peeled
- 2 stems fresh lemon grass, white part only, bruised

1 Place beef in a medium bowl. Process garlic, ginger, five-spice and oyster sauce until a smooth paste forms; season well. Add to beef; stir to coat. Cover; refrigerate for 20 minutes.

2 Heat half the oil in a large heavy-based saucepan or flameproof casserole dish over medium heat. Add half the beef; cook, stirring, for 5 minutes or until browned. Transfer to a bowl. Repeat with remaining oil and beef.

3 Add stock to pan, scrapping the bottom with a wooden spoon to remove any bits stuck on bottom of pan. Add vegetables and lemon grass; bring to the boil. Reduce heat to medium; simmer for 20 minutes or until vegetables are tender. Add beef and cook for a further 5 minutes for medium or until cooked to your liking.

4 Serve hotpot topped with beans prouts, thai basil leaves and thinly sliced fresh red chilli, if you like.

do ahead The hotpot can be prepared to the end of step 3 the day before serving, then refrigerated in an airtight container and reheated just before serving.

serving suggestion Serve hotpot with grilled bread, crusty bread rolls, steamed rice or fresh wide rice noodles.

BRAISED ITALIAN LAMB *WITH GNOCCHI*

PREP + COOK TIME 45 MINUTES **SERVES** 4

- ⅓ cup (80ml) olive oil
- 500g (1lb) lamb tenderloins, cut into 2cm (¾in) pieces
- 2 small eggplants (460g), sliced (see tip)
- 1 medium onion (150g), chopped finely
- 2 small carrots (140g), chopped finely
- 1 medium fennel bulb (300g), chopped finely
- 2 tablespoons tomato paste
- 400g (12½oz) canned diced tomatoes
- 2¼ cups (560ml) water
- ½ cup (60g) sicillian green olives, seeded
- 2 tablespoons baby capers, rinsed
- ¼ cup (60ml) red wine vinegar
- ⅓ cup (75g) fresh dates, pitted, chopped coarsely
- 500g (1lb) potato gnocchi
- ⅓ cup (25g) finely grated parmesan
- fresh basil leaves, to serve

1 Heat 1 tablespoon of the oil in a flameproof casserole dish or large heavy-based saucepan over high heat. Add lamb; cook for 1 minute on each side or until dark brown and caramelised (lamb will still be pink in the centre at this stage). Transfer to a plate.

2 Add 2 tablespoons oil to pan; cook eggplant for 5 minutes or until golden and softened. Transfer to a plate lined with paper towel to drain.

3 Add remaining oil to pan; cook onion, carrot and fennel over high heat for 5 minutes or until starting to soften and turn golden.

4 Reduce heat to medium–high, stir in tomato paste; cook for 1 minute or until fragrant. Add tomatoes, 1¾ cups of the water, olives, capers, vinegar and dates. Bring to the boil, reduce heat to low; cook, covered, for 10 minutes or until vegetables are tender and sauce is reduced and thickened.

5 Stir in gnocchi, lamb, eggplant and remaining water; cook over high heat for 5 minutes or until gnocchi and lamb are tender and eggplant is warmed through. Season to taste.

6 Serve topped with parmesan and basil.

tip You can use 1 sliced red capsicum (bell pepper) instead of the eggplant, if you like.

do ahead The stew can be prepared up to the end of step 4 up to 2 days in advance, then refrigerated in an airtight container. Reheat, then continue with the recipe just before serving.

Glossary

ALLSPICE also known as pimento or jamaican pepper; so-named because it tastes like a combination of nutmeg, cumin, clove and cinnamon. Available whole or ground.

ALMONDS

flaked paper-thin slices.

slivered small pieces cut lengthways.

ANCHOVIES small oily fish. Anchovy fillets are preserved and packed in oil or salt in small cans or jars, and are strong in flavour. Fresh anchovies are much milder in flavour.

BARLEY a nutritious grain used in soups and stews. Hulled barley, the least processed, is high in fibre. Pearl barley has had the husk removed then been steamed and polished so that only the 'pearl' of the original grain remains, much the same as white rice.

BAY LEAVES aromatic leaves from the bay tree available fresh or dried; adds a strong, slightly peppery flavour.

BEANS

black also called turtle beans or black kidney beans; an earthy-flavoured dried bean completely different from the better-known Chinese black beans (fermented soybeans). Used mostly in Mexican and South American cooking.

borlotti also called roman beans or pink beans, can be eaten fresh or dried. Interchangeable with pinto beans due to their similarity in appearance — pale pink or beige with dark red streaks.

broad (fava) available dried, fresh, canned and frozen. Fresh should be peeled twice (discarding both the outer long green pod and the beige-green tough inner shell); the frozen beans have had their pods removed but the beige shell still needs removal.

green also known as french or string beans (although the tough string they once had has generally been bred out of them), this long thin fresh bean is consumed in its entirety once cooked.

kidney medium-size red bean, slightly floury in texture yet sweet in flavour; sold dried or canned, it's found in bean mixes and is used in chilli con carne.

sprouts also known as bean shoots; tender new growths of assorted beans and seeds germinated for consumption.

BEETROOT (BEETS) firm, round root vegetable.

BICARBONATE OF SODA (BAKING SODA) a raising agent.

BREADCRUMBS

panko also known as japanese breadcrumbs. They are available in two types: larger pieces and fine crumbs. Both have a lighter texture than Western-style breadcrumbs.

stale one- or two-day-old bread made into crumbs by blending or processing.

BROCCOLINI a cross between broccoli and chinese kale; it has long asparagus-like stems with a long loose floret, both are edible. Resembles broccoli but is milder and sweeter in taste.

BUK CHOY also known as buk choy, pak choi, chinese white cabbage or chinese chard; has a fresh, mild mustard taste. Use both stems and leaves. Baby buk choy, also known as pak kat farang or shanghai buk choy, is smaller and more tender than buk choy.

BUTTER use salted or unsalted (sweet) butter; 125g is equal to one stick of butter (4oz).

BUTTERMILK originally the term given to the slightly sour liquid left after butter was churned from cream, today it is made from no-fat or low-fat milk to which specific bacterial cultures have been added. Despite its name, it is actually low in fat.

CAPERS grey-green buds of a warm climate shrub (usually Mediterranean); sold dried and salted or pickled in a vinegar brine. Baby capers are very small and have a fuller flavour. Rinse well before using.

CAPSICUM (BELL PEPPER) also called pepper. Comes in many colours: red, green, yellow, orange and purplish-black. Be sure to discard seeds and membranes before use.

CARDAMOM a spice native to India and used extensively in its cuisine; can be purchased in pod, seed or ground form. Has a distinctive aromatic, sweetly rich flavour.

CASHEWS plump, kidney-shaped, golden-brown nuts having a distinctive sweet, buttery flavour and containing about 48% fat. Because of this high fat content, they should be kept, sealed tightly, under refrigeration to avoid becoming rancid. We use unsalted cashews in this book, unless otherwise stated; they're available from health-food stores and most supermarkets.

CAVOLO NERO (TUSCAN CABBAGE) has long, narrow, wrinkled leaves and a rich and astringent, mild cabbage flavour. It doesn't lose its volume like silver beet or spinach when cooked, but it does need longer cooking.

CELERIAC (CELERY ROOT) tuberous root with knobbly brown skin, white flesh and a celery-like flavour. Keep peeled celeriac in acidulated water to stop it discolouring. It can be grated and eaten raw in salads; used in soups and stews; boiled and mashed like potatoes; or sliced thinly and deep-fried as chips.

CHEESE

cheddar the most common cow's milk 'tasty' cheese; should be aged, hard and have a pronounced bite.

fetta Greek in origin; a crumbly textured goat- or sheep-milk cheese having a sharp, salty taste. Ripened and stored in salted whey.

goat's made from goat's milk, has an earthy, strong taste; available in both soft and firm textures, in various shapes and sizes, and sometimes rolled in ash or herbs.

gruyère a hard-rind Swiss cheese with small holes and a nutty, slightly salty flavour. A popular cheese for soufflés.

haloumi a firm, cream-coloured sheep-milk cheese matured in brine; haloumi can be grilled or fried, briefly, without breaking down. Should be eaten while still warm as it becomes tough and rubbery on cooling.

mozzarella a delicate, semi-soft, white cheese traditionally made from buffalo milk. Sold fresh, it spoils rapidly so will only keep, refrigerated in brine, for 1 or 2 days at the most.

paneer a fresh unripened cow's-milk cheese, originating in India, that is similar to pressed ricotta. It has no added salt and doesn't melt at normal cooking temperatures. Available in many major supermarketsand from Indian food stores.

parmesan also called parmigiano; is a hard, grainy cow-milk cheese originating in Italy. Reggiano is the best variety.

pecorino the Italian generic name for cheeses made from sheep milk; hard, white to pale-yellow in colour. If you can't find it, use parmesan instead.

ricotta a soft, sweet, moist, white cow-milk cheese with a low fat content and a slightly grainy texture.

pizza cheese a commercial blend of varying proportions of processed grated mozzarella, cheddar and parmesan.

CHICKPEAS (GARBANZO BEANS) an irregularly round, sandy-coloured legume. Has a firm texture even after cooking, a floury mouth-feel and robust nutty flavour; available canned or dried (soak for several hours in cold water before use).

CHILLI available in many different types and sizes. Use rubber gloves when seeding and chopping fresh chillies as they can burn your skin. Removing seeds and membranes lessens the heat level.

cayenne pepper a long, thin-fleshed, extremely hot red chilli usually sold dried and ground.

jalapeño chillies once they've been dried and smoked. Having a deep, intensely smokey flavour, rather than a searing heat, chipotles are dark brown, almost black in colour and wrinkled in appearance.

flakes also sold as crushed chilli; dehydrated deep-red extremely fine slices and whole seeds.

green any unripened chilli; also some particular varieties that are ripe when green, such as jalapeño, habanero, poblano or serrano.

long available both fresh and dried; a generic term used for any moderately hot, thin, long (6-8cm/2¼-3¼ inch) chilli.

CHINESE COOKING WINE also known as shao hsing or chinese rice wine; made from fermented rice, wheat, sugar and salt with a 13.5% alcohol content. Inexpensive and found in Asian food shops.

CHINESE FIVE-SPICE POWDER although the ingredients vary from country to country, five-spice is usually a fragrant mixture of ground cinnamon, cloves, star anise, sichuan pepper and fennel seeds. Used in Chinese and other Asian cooking.

CHIVES related to the onion and leek; has a subtle onion flavour. Used more for flavour than as an cooking ingredient; chopped finely, they're good in sauces, dressings, omelettes or as a garnish.

CHORIZO a sausage of Spanish origin; made of coarsely ground pork and highly seasoned with garlic and chilli. They are deeply smoked, very spicy, and are available dry-cured or raw (which needs cooking).

CHOY SUM also known as pakaukeo or flowering cabbage, a member of the buk choy family; easy to identify with its long stems, light green leaves and yellow flowers. Stems and leaves are both edible, steamed or stir-fried.

COCONUT MILK not the liquid found inside the fruit (coconut water), but the diluted liquid from the second pressing of the white flesh of a mature coconut (the first pressing produces coconut cream). Available in cans and cartons at most supermarkets.

CORIANDER also known as pak chee, cilantro or chinese parsley; a bright-green leafy herb with a pungent flavour. Both stems and roots of coriander are also used in cooking; wash well before using. Also available ground or as seeds; these should not be substituted for fresh coriander as the tastes are completely different.

CORNFLOUR (CORNSTARCH) thickening agent available in two forms: 100% corn (maize), which is gluten free, and a wheaten cornflour (made from wheat) which is not.

CORNICHON French for gherkin, a very small variety of cucumber. Pickled, they are a traditional accompaniment to pâté; the Swiss always serve them with fondue (or raclette).

COS LETTUCE also known as romaine.

COUSCOUS a fine, grain-like cereal product made from semolina. Used mainly in Middle Eastern cooking.

CREAM

pouring also called pure, fresh or single cream. It has no additives and contains a minimum fat content of 35%.

sour a thick commercially-cultured soured cream with a 35% fat content.

thickened (heavy) a whipping cream that contains a thickener. It has a minimum fat content of 35%.

CUCUMBER, LEBANESE short, slender and thin-skinned. Probably the most popular variety because of its tender, edible skin, tiny, yielding seeds, and sweet, fresh taste.

CUMIN also known as zeera or comino; has a spicy, nutty flavour.

CURRY POWDER a blend of ground spices used for convenience. Choose mild or hot to suit your taste.

DAIKON also called white radish; this long, white horseradish has a wonderful, sweet flavour.

DUKKAH is an Egyptian spice blend made with roasted nuts and aromatic spices. It is available from Middle-Eastern food stores, specialty spice stores and some supermarkets.

EDAMAME (SHELLED SOY BEANS) available frozen from Asian food stores and some supermarkets.

EGGPLANT also called aubergine. Ranging in size from tiny to very large and in colour from pale green to deep purple.

FENNEL also known as finocchio or anise; a white to very pale green-white, firm, crisp, roundish vegetable about 8-12cm in diameter. The bulb has a slightly sweet, anise flavour but the leaves have a much stronger taste. Also the name of dried seeds having a licorice flavour.

FISH FILLETS, FIRM WHITE blue eye, bream, flathead, swordfish, ling, whiting, jewfish, snapper or sea perch are all good choices. Check for small pieces of bone and use tweezers to remove them.

FLOUR

plain (all-purpose) a general all-purpose wheat flour.

rice very fine, almost powdery, gluten-free flour; made from ground white rice. Used in baking, as a thickener, and in some Asian noodles and desserts..

FREEKEH is cracked roasted green wheat and can be found in some larger supermarkets, health food and specialty food stores.

GAI LAN also known as chinese broccoli, gai larn, kanah, gai lum and chinese kale; used more for its stems than its coarse leaves.

GARAM MASALA a blend of spices that includes cardamom, cinnamon, coriander, cloves, fennel and cumin. Black pepper and chilli can be added for heat.

GHEE a type of clarified butter used in Indian cooking; milk solids are cooked until golden brown, which imparts a nutty flavour and sweet aroma; it can be heated to a high temperature without burning.

GINGER

fresh also called green or root ginger; thick gnarled root of a tropical plant.

ground also called powdered ginger; used as a flavouring in baking but cannot be substituted for fresh ginger.

pickled pink or red in colour, paper-thin shavings of ginger pickled in a mixture of vinegar, sugar and natural colouring. Available from Asian food shops.

HONEY the variety sold in a squeezable container is not suitable for the recipes in this book.

KALE a type of leafy cabbage, rich in nutrients and vitamins. Leaf colours can range from green to violet.

KECAP MANIS see sauces, soy.

LEMON GRASS a tall, clumping, lemon-smelling and -tasting, sharp-edged grass; the white part of the stem is used, finely chopped, in cooking.

LENTILS (red, brown, yellow) dried pulses often identified by and named after their colour; also known as dhal.

LSA a ground mixture of linseeds (L), sunflower seeds (S) and almonds (A); available from supermarkets and health food stores.

MAPLE SYRUP, PURE distilled from the sap of sugar maple trees found only in Canada and the USA. Maple-flavoured syrup or pancake syrup is not an adequate substitute for the real thing

MIRIN a Japanese champagne-coloured cooking wine; made of glutinous rice and alcohol and used expressly for cooking. Should not be confused with sake.

MISO Japan's famous bean paste made from fermented soya beans and rice, rye or barley. It varies in colour, texture and saltiness. Available from supermarkets.

MUSHROOMS

button small, cultivated white mushrooms with a mild flavour. When a recipe in this book calls for an unspecified type of mushroom, use button.

porcini also known as cèpes; the richest-flavoured mushrooms. Expensive, but because they're so strongly flavoured, only a small amount is required.

portobello are mature, fully opened swiss browns; they are larger and bigger in flavour.

shiitake when fresh are also known as chinese black, forest or golden oak mushrooms; although cultivated, they are large and meaty and have the earthiness and taste of wild mushrooms. When dried, they are known as donko or dried chinese mushrooms; rehydrate before use.

swiss brown also known as cremini or roman mushrooms; are light brown mushrooms with a full-bodied flavour.

MUSTARD

dijon pale brown, creamy, distinctively flavoured, fairly mild French mustard.

wholegrain also known as seeded. A French-style coarse-grain mustard made from crushed mustard seeds and dijon-style french mustard.

NORI a type of dried seaweed used as a flavouring, garnish or for sushi. Sold in thin sheets, plain or toasted (yaki-nori).

NUTMEG a strong and pungent spice ground from the dried nut of an evergreen tree native to Indonesia. Usually found ground but the flavour is more intense from a whole nut, available from spice shops, so it's best to grate your own.

OIL

cooking spray we use a cholesterol-free cooking spray made from canola oil.

grapeseed comes from grape seeds.

olive made from ripened olives. Extra virgin and virgin are the first and second press, respectively, of the olives; "light" refers to taste not fat levels.

peanut pressed from ground peanuts; most commonly used oil in Asian cooking because of its high smoke point (capacity to handle high heat without burning).

sesame used as a flavouring rather than a cooking medium.

vegetable oils sourced from plant rather than animal fats.

ONIONS

green also known as scallion or, incorrectly, shallot; an immature onion picked before the bulb has formed. Has a long, bright-green edible stalk.

red also known as spanish, red spanish or bermuda onion; a sweet-flavoured, large, purple-red onion.

shallots also called french shallots, golden shallots or eschalots; small, brown-skinned, elongated members of the onion family.

PAPRIKA ground, dried, sweet red capsicum (bell pepper); there are many types available, including sweet, hot, mild and smoked.

PEPITAS (PUMPKIN SEED KERNELS) pale green kernels of dried pumpkin seeds; they can be bought plain or salted.

PINE NUTS not a nut but a small, cream-coloured kernel from pine cones. Toast before use to bring out their flavour.

PISTACHIOS green, delicately flavoured nuts inside hard off-white shells. Available salted or unsalted in their shells; you can also get them shelled.

POLENTA also known as cornmeal; a flour-like cereal made of ground corn (maize). Also the name of the dish made from it.

POMEGRANATE MOLASSES not to be confused with pomegranate syrup or grenadine (used in cocktails); pomegranate molasses is thicker, browner, and more concentrated in flavour. Buy from Middle Eastern food stores or specialty food shops.

PROSCIUTTO unsmoked italian ham; salted, air-cured and aged.

QUINOA pronounced keen-wa; is the seed of a leafy plant similar to spinach. It has a delicate, slightly nutty taste and chewy texture.

flakes the grains have been rolled and flattened.

RADICCHIO a red-leafed Italian chicory with a refreshing bitter taste that's eaten raw and grilled. Comes in varieties named after their places of origin, such as round-headed Verona or long-headed Treviso.

RICE

basmati a white, fragrant long-grained rice; the grains fluff up beautifully when cooked. It should be washed several times before cooking.

black high in nutritional value; the grain has a similar amount of fibre to brown rice and, like brown rice, has a mild, nutty taste.

brown retains the high-fibre, nutritious bran coating that's removed from white rice when hulled. It takes longer to cook than white rice and has a chewier texture. Once cooked, the long grains stay separate, while the short grains are soft and stickier.

RIGATONI a form of tube-shaped pasta. it is larger than penne and is usually ridged, the end doesn't terminate at an angle, like penne does.

ROCKET also known as arugula, rugula and rucola; a peppery-tasting green leaf that can be used similarly to baby spinach leaves. Baby rocket leaves are both smaller and less peppery.

SAFFRON available ground or in strands; imparts a yellow-orange colour to food once infused. The quality can vary greatly; the best is the most expensive spice in the world.

SAMBAL OELEK (also ulek or olek) Indonesian in origin; a salty paste made from ground chillies and vinegar.

SAUCES

black bean a Chinese sauce made from fermented soya beans, spices, water and wheat flour.

char siu a Chinese barbecue sauce made from sugar, water, salt, fermented soya bean paste, honey, soy sauce, malt syrup and spices. It can be found at most supermarkets.

fish called nam pla or nuoc nam; made from pulverised salted fermented fish, most often anchovies. Has a pungent smell and strong taste, so use sparingly.

hoisin a thick, sweet and spicy Chinese sauce made from salted fermented soya beans, onions and garlic.

kecap manis a thick soy sauce with added sugar and spices. The sweetness is derived from the addition of molasses or palm sugar.

oyster Asian in origin, this rich, brown sauce is made from oysters and their brine, cooked with salt and soy sauce, and thickened with starches.

soy made from fermented soya beans. Several variations are available in most supermarkets and Asian food stores.

japanese soy an all-purpose low-sodium soy sauce made with more wheat content than its Chinese counterparts.

light soy a fairly thin, pale but salty tasting sauce; used in dishes in which the natural colour of the ingredients is to be maintained. Do not confuse with salt-reduced or low-sodium soy sauces.

sweet chilli a mild sauce made from red chillies, sugar, garlic and vinegar.

worcestershire thin, dark-brown spicy sauce developed by the British when in India; used as a seasoning for meat, gravies and cocktails, and as a condiment.

SESAME SEEDS black and white are the most common of this small oval seed, however there are also red and brown varieties.

SILVER BEET also known as swiss chard; often mistakenly called spinach.

SUGAR

brown very soft, finely granulated sugar retaining molasses for its characteristic colour and flavour.

caster also known as superfine or finely granulated table sugar.

palm also known as nam tan pip, jaggery, jawa or gula melaka; made from the sap of the sugar palm tree. Light brown to black in colour and usually sold in rock-hard cakes. Substitute with brown sugar if unavailable.

white coarsely granulated table sugar, also known as crystal sugar.

SUMAC a purple-red, astringent spice ground from berries growing on shrubs flourishing wild around the Mediterranean; adds a tart, lemony flavour to food. Available from major supermarkets.

TAHINI a rich, sesame-seed paste.

TAMARI a thick, dark soy sauce made mainly from soya beans, but without the wheat; used in most standard soy sauces.

TAMARIND CONCENTRATE (OR PASTE) the distillation of tamarind pulp into a condensed, compacted paste. Thick and purple-black, it requires no soaking. Found in Asian food stores.

TEMPEH a traditional soy product originating from Indonesia. It is made by a natural culturing and controlled fermentation process that binds soybeans into a cake form.

TOFU also called bean curd; an off-white, custard-like product made from the "milk" of crushed soybeans. Comes fresh as soft or firm, and processed as fried or pressed dried sheets.

VINEGAR

balsamic originally from Modena, Italy, there are now many balsamic vinegars on the market ranging in pungency and quality depending on how long they have been aged. Is a deep rich brown colour and has a sweet and sour flavour.

cider made from fermented apples.

red wine based on fermented red wine.

rice a colourless vinegar made from fermented rice, sugar and salt. Also known as seasoned rice vinegar.

white wine made from white wine.

VIETNAMESE MINT not a mint at all, but a pungent and peppery narrow-leafed member of the buckwheat family.

WATERCRESS one of the cress family, a large group of peppery greens. Highly perishable, so must be used as soon as possible after purchase.

WOMBOK (NAPA CABBAGE) also known as peking or chinese cabbage. Elongated in shape with pale green, crinkly leaves.

WONTON WRAPPERS made of flour, egg and water, are found in the refrigerated or freezer section of Asian food shops and many supermarkets. These come in different thicknesses and shapes.

YOGHURT, GREEK-STYLE plain yoghurt strained in a cloth (muslin) to remove the whey and to give it a creamy consistency.

Conversion Chart

Measures

One Australian metric measuring cup holds approximately 250ml; one Australian metric tablespoon holds 20ml; one Australian metric teaspoon holds 5ml.

The difference between one country's measuring cups and another's is within a two- or three-teaspoon variance, and will not affect your cooking results. North America, New Zealand and the United Kingdom use a 15ml tablespoon.

All cup and spoon measurements are level. The most accurate way of measuring dry ingredients is to weigh them. When measuring liquids, use a clear glass or plastic jug with the metric markings.

The imperial measurements used in these recipes are approximate only. Measurements for cake pans are approximate only. Using same-shaped cake pans of a similar size should not affect the outcome of your baking. We measure the inside top of the cake pan to determine sizes.

We use large eggs with an average weight of 60g.

Dry Measures

METRIC	IMPERIAL
15G	½OZ
30G	1OZ
60G	2OZ
90G	3OZ
125G	4OZ (¼LB)
155G	5OZ
185G	6OZ
220G	7OZ
250G	8OZ (½LB)
280G	9OZ
315G	10OZ
345G	11OZ
375G	12OZ (¾LB)
410G	13OZ
440G	14OZ
470G	15OZ
500G	16OZ (1LB)
750G	24OZ (1½LB)
1KG	32OZ (2LB)

Liquid Measures

METRIC	IMPERIAL
30ML	1 FLUIDoz
60ML	2 FLUIDoz
100ML	3 FLUIDoz
125ML	4 FLUIDoz
150ML	5 FLUIDoz
190ML	6 FLUIDoz
250ML	8 FLUIDoz
300ML	10 FLUIDoz
500ML	16 FLUIDoz
600ML	20 FLUIDoz
1000ML (1 LITRE)	1¾ PINTS

Length Measures

METRIC	IMPERIAL
3MM	⅛IN
6MM	¼IN
1CM	½IN
2CM	¾IN
2.5CM	1IN
5CM	2IN
6CM	2½IN
8CM	3IN
10CM	4IN
13CM	5IN
15CM	6IN
18CM	7IN
20CM	8IN
22CM	9IN
25CM	10IN
28CM	11IN
30CM	12IN (1FT)

Oven Temperatures

The oven temperatures in this book are for conventional ovens; if you have a fan-forced oven, decrease the temperature by 10–20 degrees.

	°C (CELSIUS)	°F (FAHRENHEIT)
VERY SLOW	120	250
SLOW	150	300
MODERATELY SLOW	160	325
MODERATE	180	350
MODERATELY HOT	200	400
HOT	220	425
VERY HOT	240	475

INDEX

A

almond crumble, tamari 50
apple slaw 174
asian greens, steamed 148
avocado cream 111

B

beans
    black bean lamb & broccolini stir-fry 64
    butter bean hummus 191
    garlicky 147
beef
    beef & carrot hot pot, vietnamese 228
    beef & porcini mushroom stew with parmesan mash 212
    bibimbap 58
    chargrilled steak, mushroom & beetroot salad 103
    chilli con carne cornbread pie 137
    creamy beef & mushroom pasta with kale chips 24
    cuban beef empanadas with cinnamon roast pumpkin 157
    fast beef burgundy with pasta 12
    grilled beef & broccolini salad 120
    hoisin beef & shiitake stir-fry 79
    Indian-spiced roast, & root vegetables 188
    lemon grass beef noodle salad 53
    mexican pulled 207
    roast beef bourguignon 183
    tex mex steak salad fajitas 88
bibimbap 58
bread
    baguette monsieur 27
    garlic bagels 26
    haloumi, herb & garlic naan 27
    pizza loaf 26
buttermilk scones 220

C

capsicum paste, smoky 31
cauliflower
    dukkah-crumbed lamb cutlets & roasted cauliflower salad 119
    miso-roasted whole cauliflower with spring veg salad 187
    'rice' pilaf 63
cavolo nero colcannon 154
chermoulla chicken, barbecued with fattoush 116
chicken
    baked chicken, pea & ricotta meatballs with spaghetti 36
    baked 'claypot' chicken with ginger & green onion 145
    barbecued chermoulla chicken with fattoush 116
    butter chicken, healthy 204
    char-grilled peach chicken 215
    chicken & corn enchilada bake 134
    chicken & thyme one-pan pie 133
    chicken fricasee, autumn with buttermilk scones 220
    chicken 'n' chips, roasted 162
    chicken paprikash with egg noodles 23
    chicken parmigiana bake 130
    chicken saltimbocca tortellini 35
    chicken satay skewers with crunchy rainbow salad 84
    chicken wonton noodle soup 224
    easy roast chicken dinner with inside-out stuffing 173
    japanese crumbed chicken, edamame & brown rice salad 112
    mexican chicken salad 92
    roast chimichurri chicken with pan 'unstuffing' 169
    sticky chicken with zucchini 'noodles' 57
    sticky wings with quinoa 'fried rice' 165
    stir-fried, with tamari almond crumble 50
    summer spaghetti with chicken 39
    Thai-style chicken filled omelettes 75
    wontons 224
chickpea
    croûtons 100
    za'atar chickpeas 216

chilli con carne cornbread pie 137
chimichurri 169
coconut rice 62
couscous, lemon pistachio 219
cucumber & mint pickle 54
curry
    butter chicken, healthy 204
    lamb & potato with cucumber & mint pickle 54
    super-green vegetable 196

D

dressing
    balsamic & garlic 106
    buttermilk 115
    creamy ranch 107
    french 106
    herb 120
    tahini herb 107
dukkah-crumbed lamb cutlets & roasted cauliflower salad 119

E

empanadas, cuban beef with cinnamon roast pumpkin 157

F

fattoush 116
fennel & orange salt roast pork with beetroot & orange salad 166
fetta & spinach-stuffed lamb with roasted veg 177
fish see also ocean trout; salmon; tuna
    baked fish 'n' chips with yoghurt tartare 153
    'fish & chip' salad with tartare dressing 91
    fragrant fish & green tea noodle parcels 180
    jerk fish & slaw salad cups 111
    mediterranean fish 'pie' 150

G

gado gado tempeh stir-fry lettuce cups 67

ginger
  ginger–green onion sauce 145
  ginger rice, steamed 62
gnocchi, braised italian lamb 231

H

hungarian goulash soup 227

I

Indian-spiced roast beef & root
  vegetables 188

J

jerk fish & slaw salad cups 111

K

kale chips 24
kashmiri lamb skewers & paneer salad
  123

L

lamb
  barbecued lamb, black rice & kale
    salad 108
  black bean lamb & broccolini stir-fry
    64
  braised italian lamb with gnocchi 231
  dukkah-crumbed lamb cutlets &
    roasted cauliflower salad 119
  fast moroccan roast, with butter
    bean hummus 191
  fetta & spinach-stuffed lamb with
    roasted veg 177
  kashmiri lamb skewers 123
  lamb & haloumi skewers with roasted
    vegetable & barley salad 104
  lamb & mint meatballs with risoni 200
  lamb & potato 'curry' with cucumber
    & mint pickle 54
  lamb & rosemary ragout, fast with
    orecchiette 20
  nut-crumbed lamb racks with
    hasselback roast veg 184
  oregano lamb, potato & fetta parcels
    138

(lamb continued)
  roast lamb shawarma with warm
    carrot salad 192
  spaghetti with lebanese-spiced
    lamb & pine nuts 28
  spiced lamb & quinoa biryani with
    coriander yoghurt 68
  spiced lamb pilaf with almonds &
    currants 208
lemon grass beef noodle salad 53
lemon pistachio couscous 219
lentil spaghetti 'bolognese' 8

M

mac 'n' cheese, loaded veg 15
mango chutney yoghurt 179
mexican
  chicken salad 92
  pulled beef 207
mint sauce 179
miso
  miso ocean trout hot pot 199
  miso-roasted whole cauliflower
    with spring veg salad 187
  miso salmon & stir-fried greens with
    soba noodles 76
moroccan roast lamb, fast, with butter
  bean hummus 191
mushrooms
  beef & porcini mushroom stew with
    parmesan mash 212
  creamy beef & mushroom pasta
    with kale chips 24
  creamy mushroom sauce 178
  hoisin beef & shiitake stir-fry 79
mustard vinaigrette 103

N

nasi goreng, brown rice 46

O

ocean trout
  miso ocean trout hot pot 199
  soy-glazed, sushi salad bowl 87
  walnut-dukkah ocean trout with
    tahini yoghurt sauce 170
omelettes, Thai-style chicken filled 75

onion tarte tatin, red, with crunchy nut
  topping 126

P

pasta
  baked chicken, pea & ricotta
    meatballs with spaghetti 36
  breakfast-for-dinner pasta 43
  cheat's pork & fennel lasagne 141
  chicken paprikash with egg noodles 23
  chicken saltimbocca tortellini 35
  creamy beef & mushroom pasta
    with kale chips 24
  fast beef burgundy with pasta 12
  lamb & mint meatballs with risoni 200
  lamb & rosemary ragout, fast with
    orecchiette 20
  linguine with garlic prawns & chorizo
    16
  mac 'n' cheese, loaded veg 15
  pasta with smoky pork, capsicum &
    rocket 31
  penne with roasted pumpkin,
    asparagus & pepita pesto 19
  spaghetti lentil 'bolognese' 8
  spaghetti with lebanese-spiced
    lamb & pine nuts 28
  spinach & ricotta stuffed pasta shell
    bake 146
  spring vegetable pasta with minty
    pea pesto 32
  summer spaghetti with chicken 39
  tuna & chilli pasta with dukkah
    crumbs 11
  warm minestrone pasta salad 40
pea
  pea pesto, minty 32
  peas & parmesan crunch 148
pepita pesto 19
pies
  chicken & thyme one-pan 133
  chilli con carne cornbread 137
  mediterranean fish 150
polenta, soft 129, 219
pork
  cheat's mushu pork 49
  fennel & orange salt roast, with
    beetroot & orange salad 166

(pork continued)

herb & mustard pork loaded potato salad 99

lime-ginger pork stir-fry with sweet chilli dressing 71

oven-barbecued ribs with apple slaw 174

paprika pork skewers with herby potato pork salad 96

pasta with smoky pork, capsicum & rocket 31

pork adobo 211

pork & fennel lasagne, cheat's 141

pork, crackling & pear tray bake with cavolo nero colcannon 154

tamarind-honey pork & pineapple with rice noodle salad 61

potatoes

herby yoghurt potato salad 96

paprika potato wedges 146

parmesan mash 212

puree 218

prawns

five-spice salt & pepper prawn stir-fry 80

linguine with garlic prawns & chorizo 16

prawn, asparagus & pea quinoa risotto 203

sesame prawn 'toast' noodle salad 95

pumpkin soup, chai-roasted with whipped paneer toasts 223

Q

quinoa

'fried rice' 165

pine nut & parsley 217

prawn, asparagus & pea quinoa risotto 203

spiced lamb & quinoa biryani with coriander yoghurt 68

R

raita 123

rice

basmati pilaf 63

brown rice nasi goreng 46

coconut 62

ginger rice, steamed 62

rice noodle salad 61

(rice continued)

seafood paella bake 158

soy-glazed ocean trout sushi salad bowl 87

spiced lamb pilaf with almonds & currants 208

rocket & lemon pesto 39

S

sage & onion gravy 178

salads

apple slaw 174

barbecued lamb, black rice & kale 108

chargrilled steak, mushroom & beetroot 103

chicken & avocado club salad 115

fattoush 116

grilled beef & broccolini 120

herb & mustard pork loaded potato 99

herby yoghurt potato 96

japanese crumbed chicken, edamame & brown rice 112

kashmiri lamb skewers & paneer 123

mexican chicken 92

rice noodle 61

roasted vegetable & barley 104

sesame prawn 'toast' noodle 95

slaw 111

spring veg 187

vermicelli 53

warm minestrone pasta salad 40

salmon

miso salmon & stir-fried greens with soba noodles 76

salmon niçoise tray bake 142

salsa verde 142

satay sauce 84

sausage agrodolce & polenta bake 129

seafood paella bake 158

semi-dried tomato pesto 40

shawarma, roast lamb with warm carrot salad 192

soup

chicken wonton noodle 224

hungarian goulash 227

pumpkin chai-roasted with whipped paneer toasts 223

spinach & ricotta stuffed pasta shell bake 146

spring vegetable

pasta with minty pea pesto 32

salad 187

stir-fries

black bean lamb & broccolini 64

chicken with tamari almond crumble 50

five-spice salt & pepper prawn 80

gado gado tempeh stir-fry lettuce cups 67

hoisin beef & shiitake 79

lime-ginger pork, with sweet chilli dressing 71

miso salmon & stir-fried greens with soba noodles 76

salt & pepper tofu with sugar snap pea 72

soy-glazed ocean trout sushi salad bowl 87

tex mex steak salad fajitas 88

tomato & avocado 137

sweet potato chips 162

T

tagine, vegetable with za'atar chickpeas 216

tahini

tahini herb dressing 107

tahini-yoghurt sauce 170

tamarind-honey pork & pineapple with rice noodle salad 61

tarte tatin, red onion with crunchy nut topping 126

tex mex steak salad fajitas 88

tofu, salt & pepper with sugar snap pea stir-fry 72

tomato & avocado salad 137

tuna & chilli pasta with dukkah crumbs 11

W

walnut-dukkah ocean trout with tahini yoghurt sauce 170

wontons, chicken 224

Y

yoghurt tartare 153

Z

zucchini

'spaghetti' & baked fetta salad with chickpea croûtons 100

sticky chicken with zucchini 'noodles' 57